The Wise Shall Realize

A translation of
A selection of Gautama Supreme Buddha's discourses
from the Pāli Canon, delivered by
Most Venerable Kiribathgoda Gnānānanda Thera

The Wise Shall Realize

Most Venerable Kiribathgoda Gnānānanda Thera

© All Rights Reserved
ISBN : 978-955-687-055-8

1st Print: Binara Full Moon Poyaday - 2556 B.E. (Sep. 2012)

Computer Typesetting and Cover Page by
Mahamevnawa Monastery
Markham, Ontario, Canada L6C 1P2
Telephone: 905-927-7117

Published by
Mahamegha Publishers
Waduwawa, Yatigaloluwa, Polgahawela, Sri Lanka.
Telephone: +94 37 2053300 I 77 3216685
www.mahameghapublishers.com I mahameghapublishers@gmail.com

The Wise Shall Realize

A translation of
A selection of Gautama Supreme Buddha's discourses
from the Pāli Canon, delivered by
Most Venerable Kiribathgoda Gnānānanda Thera

Publications

The Wise Shall Realize

Dedication

As there are lotuses that rise clear above the water and seek the nourishing beam of the sun, there are beings who seek the wisdom of the Supreme Buddha's Dhamma.

May they achieve the ultimate bliss of Nibbāna.

To the Reader

Undeniably, most people in this world are desperately searching for peace and happiness. Yet apart from experiencing momentary pleasure or satisfaction, nothing can provide true liberation and bliss other than the Teachings of the Supreme Buddha, *the Noble Dhamma*. By compassionately teaching about suffering, the origin of suffering, the cessation of suffering, and the path leading to the cessation of suffering, Supreme Buddha revealed the true nature of life, and illuminated the way to achieve ultimate happiness.

Mahamevnāwa is an organization of Buddhist Monasteries, established 13 years ago in Sri Lanka, for the purpose of spiritual development through Gautama Supreme Buddha's Dispensation. Its founder, Venerable Kiribathgoda Gnānānanda Thera, most affectionately known by his students as *'Lokuswaminwahanse'* (*Chief Monk or Teacher*), has become a highly respected and cherished Buddhist monk all over the world. At a time when the true Doctrine of the Supreme Buddha was hardly known or practised, The Chief Monk endeavoured to learn the Noble Dhamma from the 18,000 original discourses – all of which have been protected for over 2,500 years within the Pāli Canon. Having mastered the subtlety of the Dhamma, The Chief Monk began to teach it, honestly and clearly; using everyday simple language. The Chief Monk began with a small group of four eager listeners, and today pursues the same compassionate and genuine intention with crowds of up to 2,500,000. By sincerely teaching the Supreme Buddha's Dhamma in its purest form, The Chief Monk has formed an era where faithful disciples can practise the Doctrine and realize the true happiness in this very life.

There are now 60 Mahamevnāwa Monasteries, with overseas branches in India, Canada, United States, Germany, Australia,

England, and the United Arab Emirates (Dubai). Nearly 600 Monks have been ordained, and practise under The Chief Monk's guidance. These Monks share the same humble ambition to teach the true and sublime Dhamma. This book represents a collection of sermons which explain several original discourses (*suttas*). The sermons were delivered by The Chief Monk and have been transcribed into print to allow for quiet reflection and wise consideration. Its rich content will help the reader to understand the extraordinary qualities of Supreme Buddha and thereby develop confidence in the Buddha's wisdom, as well as gain an understanding of more advanced concepts like dependent-arising and mind training.

"Mankind's wonderful treasure of wisdom is the Teachings of the Supreme Buddha. This Noble Doctrine, the Dhamma, illuminates our lives, bringing happiness and joy. Go in search of this wonderful Dhamma, lead your life accordingly, eradicate suffering, and join that fortunate band of people who experience the Supreme Bliss."

Venerable Kiribathgoda Gnānānanda Thera

Mahamevnāwa Buddhist Monasteries compassionately offer noble friendship and guidance to all who earnestly seek knowledge and liberation in Gautama Supreme Buddha's Dispensation. For all who read this book, may the word of the Supreme Buddha enhance your wisdom.

Lokavabodha Sutta

"Bhikkhus, the world has been fully understood by the Tathāgata; the Tathāgata is released from the world.

Bhikkhus, the origin of the world has been fully understood by the Tathāgata; the origin of the world has been eradicated by the Tathāgata.

Bhikkhus, the cessation of the world has been fully understood by the Tathāgata; the cessation of the world has been realized by the Tathāgata.

Bhikkhus, the path leading to the cessation of the world has been fully understood by the Tathāgata; the path leading to the cessation of the world has been developed by the Tathāgata.

Bhikkhus, in this world with its devas, māras and brahmās; with its recluses and brahmins, among humankind with its princes and people, whatever is seen, whatever is heard, whatever is smelled, whatever is tasted, whatever is touched, whatever is cognized, whatever is attained, whatever is sought, and whatever is comprehended, all have been fully understood by the Tathāgata .

Thus, the Blessed One is called the Tathāgata.

Bhikkhus, from the night when the Tathāgata awakened to unsurpassed Supreme Enlightenment until the night when the Tathāgata passes away into Nibbāna, with nothing remaining, whatever the Tathāgata speaks, utters, and explains, all that is just so, and not otherwise.

Thus, the Blessed One is called the Tathāgata .

Bhikkhus, as the Tathāgata says, so the Tathāgata does.
As the Tathāgata does, so the Tathāgata says.

In this way, as the Tathāgata says, so the Tathāgata does.
As the Tathāgata does, so the Tathāgata says.

Thus, the Blessed One is called the Tathāgata.

Bhikkhus, in this world, with its devas, māras, and brahmās, with its recluses and brahmins, among humankind with its princes and people, the Tathāgata is the conqueror, unvanquished, all-seer, wielding power.

Thus, the Blessed One is called the Tathāgata.

This was said by the Blessed One. So, with regard to this, it was said:

By knowledge of the whole world, the whole world as it truly is, the Blessed One is released from all the world, in all the world the Blessed One is unattached.

The all-conquering heroic sage, freed from every bond is the Blessed One; the Blessed One has reached that perfect peace, Nibbāna which is free from fear.

Rid of taints, the Blessed One is enlightened, free from suffering, and free from doubts; has destroyed all kamma, and is released by the full destruction of clinging.

Our Supreme Buddha, our Blessed One, is a lion, unsurpassed; for in the world together with its devas, the Blessed One set the Brahma-wheel in motion.

Thus those devas and human beings, gone for refuge to the Supreme Buddha, on meeting the Blessed One, pay homage - the Greatest One, free from diffidence.

i. Tamed, the Blessed One is unsurpassed in taming others.
ii. Calmed, the Blessed One is unsurpassed in calming others.
iii. Freed, the Blessed One is unsurpassed in freeing others;
iv. Crossed over, the Blessed One is unsurpassed in helping others to cross over.

Thus, they pay due homage to the Blessed One, the Greatest One free from diffidence, by saying:

"In the world together with its devas, there is no other equalling you, our Supreme Buddha."

Khuddaka Nikāya

Namo tassa Bhagavato Arahato Sammā Sambuddhassa

Homage to the Blessed One, the Worthy One,
the Supremely Enlightened One

"All have I overcome, all-knowing am I;
with regard to all things, unattached.
Having renounced all,
and released in the end of craving;
having fully comprehended on my own,
whom shall I call 'my teacher'?

The gift of Dhamma surpasses all gifts;
the taste of Dhamma, all tastes;
delight in Dhamma, all delights.
One who has destroyed craving,
vanquishes all suffering.

Gautama Supreme Buddha
Dhp 353-354

Table of Contents

᥊ *Mittāmacca Sutta*
The Real Assurance to Life

SAMYUTTA NIKĀYA 55:16

We must try to see this life for what it actually is. This human life is a very rare one, so as quickly as possible we must try to understand the reality of life through Supreme Buddha's Teachings.

The Danger of an Ordinary Life

According to Supreme Buddha's Teachings, all beings in all worlds (the human world, the heavenly world, the animal world, the ghost world and hell), can be placed into two categories. The first is ordinary people. There is grave danger with an ordinary life. Supreme Buddha explained the danger of an ordinary life. Those leading ordinary lives do not know about the Supreme Buddha, and they are not skilled in the Buddha's Teachings. They do not know how to follow the Path to escape suffering, and they do not know about the realities of life. The danger of an ordinary life is that at any moment after this life – after the dissolution of the body, they will be re-born in the animal world, in hell, or in the ghost world. That is the danger that ordinary people face after the current life. They will not be able to escape suffering.

Supreme Buddha explained that this Dhamma (Buddha's Teachings) is *for the wise, not for the unwise.* The wise refers to those who have the ambition in their lives to escape suffering. That is the key to learning Supreme Buddha's Teachings. Therefore, this is a great opportunity to understand suffering, to eradicate the cause of suffering, and to follow the Path that leads to real happiness in this very life.

The Blessings of a Noble Friend

The second category is noble people. Noble people are followers of the Supreme Buddha. The first step is to associate with noble friends. Noble friends are people who want to escape suffering and spend time thinking about how to escape suffering. They want to follow the Path taught by the Supreme Buddha to escape suffering. Those friends are called noble friends. The opportunity to hear the Dhamma is the advantage of associating with noble friends. By listening to the Dhamma, we will be able to achieve real happiness. In many of Supreme Buddha's Teachings, Buddha explained that noble friends are very rare in the world. Because noble friends are very rare, the chance to hear the Dhamma is also rare. Therefore, the opportunity to escape from suffering is *a very rare opportunity.* Before our death, we must realize this great opportunity.

Supreme Buddha explained that by developing four factors, one will be able to achieve the first stage of wisdom called the Stream Entrant *(Sotāpanna)*. This is the first stage of developing wisdom through Supreme Buddha's Teachings. Then, by developing the same four factors further, one will be able to achieve the next stage, which is called the Once-Returner *(Sakadāgāmi)*.

All conditions necessary to escape suffering depend on wisdom. By developing those same four factors even further, one will be able to achieve the next stage, which is called the Non-Returner *(Anāgāmi)*. By developing the same four factors to the highest level, one will be able to achieve the last stage, the ultimate deliverance and the goal of real happiness, the *Arahant*.

An ordinary life is very dangerous. The only things we can expect with an ordinary life are aging and death. In a noble life, a noble person as a follower of Supreme Buddha, will always try to understand suffering. *Suffering* is the fundamental truth that needs to be understood in Supreme Buddha's Teachings. There are Four Truths and they are all noble. The first Noble Truth is suffering. The noble disciple of the Supreme Buddha is trying to understand suffering, and that is *'the wisdom'*.

Earlier, we tried to understand the danger of an ordinary person. What is that danger? It is that, after death, he will be born in a bad destination. With a noble person's life, there is a very good opportunity to escape from hell, to escape from the animal world, to escape from the ghost world and to escape from all bad destinations. For that to happen, we must achieve some goals in this very life.

The Stream Entrant – *Sotāpanna*

The first goal is to achieve the Stream Entrant stage. If you can achieve that stage, Supreme Buddha, our Great Teacher, explained that you are definitely a fortunate person, and you have already escaped from all bad destinations.

First, we must develop four factors. Associating with noble friends is the first factor. Listening to Dhamma through the association of noble friends is the second factor. The third factor is developing *wise consideration* (*yonisomanasikara*), which means investigating the Dhamma through your own life and with your own wisdom. The fourth factor is following the Noble Eightfold Path. (SN 55:5)

These factors are related and dependent on each other. Without the association of noble friends, will there be the opportunity to listen to Dhamma? Never. Without listening to the Dhamma, will we be able to develop wise consideration? No. Without developing wise consideration, will we be able to follow the Path? It would be impossible. By cultivating these four factors, one can attain the Stream Entrant stage and escape from all bad destinations.

Additionally, there are four factors that define a person as a Stream Entrant. The first factor is having an *unshakeable confidence in the Supreme Buddha*. We have to understand that this is not mere faith. This is an *unshakeable* confidence obtained through the understanding of the Dhamma, the Buddha's Teachings, and applying them to one's life. Can you understand that this is not a mere belief, or ritual worship, or the chanting of some stanzas? This is a deep understanding of the reality of our lives, and it is achieved gradually. If you develop your confidence to an unshakeable level, you will have achieved the first factor of a Stream Entrant.

The second factor of a Stream Entrant is having *an unshakeable confidence in the Dhamma*, the Teachings of the Buddha. The third factor of a Stream Entrant is having *an unshakeable confidence in the Sangha*, the noble disciples of the Buddha. The fourth and last factor of a Stream Entrant is following the Five Precepts. Without breaching, and with mindfulness, you must follow the Five Precepts.

All these factors are detailed in Supreme Buddha's Teachings. In this very life, we are fortunate to have the opportunity to develop these factors. This is what we must realize and appreciate.

The Shell of Ignorance

Supreme Buddha explained that our life is like an egg. What is the nature of eggs? There is a hard shell. Supreme Buddha explained that our lives are like eggs covered with hard shells (Vinaya Pitaka). That shell is *ignorance*. Ignorance means not knowing the Four Noble Truths. Though we laugh and enjoy ourselves with many worldly things, we are still inside that shell. Because of this ignorance, upon our death we will be reborn in the animal world or hell. Without knowledge of the Buddha's Teachings, all beings in this world are in that shell. They are covered with that hard shell. And as they enjoy life, they think that they are experiencing real happiness, and it is the 'real' gratification of life. But, they do not know *real happiness*, and they do not know that they are still inside that shell of ignorance. Very rarely, does one have the opportunity to break that shell.

By breaking the shell of ignorance, we will be able to achieve *true knowledge*, called *vijjā,* in the Pāli language. *Avijjā* means *ignorance*. What is the meaning of ignorance? Not knowing the Four Noble Truths is ignorance. So, what is the meaning of true knowledge? Knowledge of the Four Noble Truths is **true knowledge.**

This is a very rare opportunity to gradually break the shell of ignorance. If you break through the shell, then real happiness will emerge. That is why Supreme Buddha explained, *"Bhikkhus, I am the First One, I am the Eldest One, I am the Greatest One to break that shell and come out"*. Buddha advised that we should also follow the same Path, for there is real happiness to be achieved, but it is outside of that shell. We have to achieve something in our lives; we have to attain something. This is not just an ordinary life, with aging and death, but a great life with an opportunity to develop our own wisdom with the help of our Great Teacher, the Supreme Buddha.

Can you remember **the four factors of a Stream Entrant**, which can be achieved in this very life? They are:

1. an unshakeable confidence in the Supreme Buddha,
2. an unshakeable confidence in the Dhamma – the Supreme Buddha's Teachings,
3. an unshakeable confidence in the Sangha – the Noble Disciples, and
4. observance of the Five Precepts, without breach.

Do not forget that this is not just confidence. It has to be an *unshakeable confidence*. To develop an unshakeable confidence, you have to gradually learn the Supreme Buddha's Teachings.

Developing an Unshakeable Confidence in the Supreme Buddha

Supreme Buddha explained that unshakeable confidence in the Supreme Buddha refers to confidence about Supreme Buddha's knowledge. Unshakeable confidence is developed based on understanding the knowledge of the Supreme Buddha. *Saddhā* means *'confidence'*. This is the Pāli term that Supreme Buddha used for *unshakeable confidence*. *Tathāgatassa bodhi* means *'the knowledge of the Supreme Buddha'*. *Saddahati tathāgatassa bodhi* means *'unshakeable confidence in the knowledge of the Supreme Buddha'*. What is that knowledge? By examining the great qualities of the Supreme Buddha, one can understand the knowledge of our Great Teacher.

Firstly, we must understand that our Great Teacher was an *Arahant*. An *Arahant* is one who has eradicated all bad conditions of the mind, which include: passion, lust, desire, hatred, ill will, delusion, and all other defilements of the mind. There should be an unshakeable confidence about that quality of our Great Teacher. That unshakeable confidence is developed by knowing that in this world, and throughout all worlds, there is no other teacher with this *Arahant* quality.

The second quality of our Teacher is *Sammā Sambuddho*. *Sammā Sambuddho* means that our Great Teacher understood the Four Noble Truths without anyone's help. So our Great Teacher is really the *one and only* Teacher. What is the significance of the Four Noble Truths? These Truths explain the realities of life. Our Great Teacher understood the realities of life, without anyone's help. By knowing this, we can establish an unshakeable confidence based on this second quality.

The third quality is *vijjācaranasampanno*. *Vijjā* means *'true knowledge'*. There are three kinds of knowledge. Firstly, the Supreme Buddha, our Great Teacher had knowledge of the past lives of beings. Through this knowledge the Supreme Buddha knew that this is a long journey through *samsāra* (the cycle of birth and death). The second knowledge our Great Teacher had was the passing away and the reappearing of beings. There should be a confidence based on both these kinds of knowledge. Because of that knowledge, we can be sure that if we do not try to achieve the Stream Entrant stage in this life, our next destination will not be a good one. The third knowledge that the Supreme Buddha had was the knowledge of the destruction of all taints (the destruction of all defilements). So, with this true knowledge, our Great Teacher had excellent virtue, excellent concentration, excellent wisdom, and excellent liberation. And that is called *vijjācaranasampanno* – the one and only Teacher in this world.

The fourth quality is *sugata*. *Su* means *'the correct path'*. *Gatha* means *'followed'*. Therefore, *sugata* means *'following the correct path'*. Supreme Buddha followed the best path, the Noble Eightfold Path, and achieved the bliss of *Nibbāna* (ultimate liberation).

The fifth quality is *lokavidu*. *Lokavidu* means *'knower of the worlds'*. It is the one who understands the origin of all worlds, understands the cessation of all worlds, and understands how to escape from all worlds.

The sixth quality is *anuttaro purisadammasārathi*. *Anuttara* means *'excellent'*. It means *'exalted'*, there is no one else. *Purisadammasārathi* means *'Buddha is the Teacher of people to be tamed'*. What is the way of taming? The Supreme Buddha's way of taming is with virtue, concentration and wisdom, and without any weapons. Even today, we are tamed by those great qualities. We are following the Path of virtue (precepts and good discipline), we are following the Path of concentration, and we are following the Path of wisdom.

The seventh quality is *satthā devamanussānam*. *Satthā devamanussānam* means *'the Teacher of gods and humans'*. We have to clearly understand that our Great Teacher is not only the Teacher of humans, but also the Teacher of gods. If we are able to achieve the Stream Entrant stage in this very life, Supreme Buddha explained that we will be re-born in the heavenly world.

The Dhamma, the Teachings of the Buddha, exists in the heavenly worlds.

The eighth quality is *Buddha*. *Buddha* means *'one who has understood the Four Noble Truths without anyone's help, and is able to proclaim the Dhamma to others'*. *Buddha* means one who teaches without holding anything back; with great compassion and with great loving kindness, so that others may understand the Four Noble Truths and achieve real happiness.

The ninth quality is *Bhagavā*. *Bhagavā* means *'the Blessed One'*. This means that our Great Teacher, is the one and only teacher who held all of these qualities. These are the great qualities of the Supreme Buddha. Because of these qualities, we can develop an unshakeable confidence in the Supreme Buddha.

There are more than 18,000 discourses of Supreme Buddha's Teachings. I am explaining these Teachings from the *original discourses*. Supreme Buddha is our Teacher and we are the followers. Supreme Buddha discovered the Path, and that is why Supreme Buddha is our Great Teacher. Step by step, by listening to those discourses and studying the Dhamma, we have the opportunity to develop the confidence in the *Arahant* quality. Over and over, we must reflect to secure that confidence. In the discourses, the supreme qualities of the Buddha are revealed.

Developing an Unshakeable Confidence in the Dhamma

The first factor of a Stream Entrant is an unshakeable confidence in our Great Teacher. The second factor is an unshakeable confidence in the Supreme Buddha's Teachings, the Dhamma. We must understand the qualities of the Supreme Buddha's Teachings. By understanding the qualities of the Dhamma, we will be able to compare it with other teachings, and we will realize that these are the *great* Teachings. We must also be able to see the difference between the original teachings of the Supreme Buddha and other misrepresentations.

The first quality of the Dhamma is *svākkhāto bhagavatā dhammo*. *Svākkhata* means that Supreme Buddha's Dhamma is well proclaimed, from beginning to end. That means that there is an excellent beginning, an excellent middle and an excellent end.

Now, let me talk about everyday science for a moment. Is there an end to science? No, it is always changing and there is no end. In Supreme Buddha's Teachings, there is a clear end. There is a very clear goal. There is a very clear aspiration. And, there is a very clear Path – the Noble Eightfold Path. Only Supreme Buddha's Teachings have these qualities. Supreme Buddha's Teachings have an excellent beginning, an excellent middle and an excellent end. What is the excellent beginning? The excellent beginning is virtue or morality. What is the excellent middle? The excellent middle is concentration. What is the excellent end? The excellent end is wisdom.

The second quality is *sanditthika*. *Sanditthika* means that this Dhamma is to be realized here and now, in this very life. That is why some have the goal of wanting to achieve *Nibbāna* in this very life. These goals are not for the next life, but are for *this* life. These goals can be attained in this very life. Other teachings do not have this quality.

The third quality is *akālika*. *Akālika* means that this Dhamma is immediately effective. If you follow the Five Precepts (virtue) at this moment, the results will be there in the next moment. If you practise concentration now, the results will be there in the next moment. If you try to obtain wisdom now, the results will be there in the next moment. There is no delay. Why is that? It is because this Dhamma is *akālika*.

Supreme Buddha has explained in the Doctrine that aging and death are because of birth. Dependent on birth, aging and death arise (Dependent Arising – *Paticca Samuppāda*). In the past, what happened with our grandmothers' and grandfathers' lives? There was aging and death because of birth. Let's think about the future, and think specifically about our sons' and daughters' lives. There will be aging and death because of birth. What is the doctrine? It is the *same* doctrine. With our own life, it is the same reality. This quality of the Dhamma is called *akālika* – it doesn't change with time.

The fourth quality is *ehipassika*. *Ehipassika* means that we can invite everyone to *come and see* this Dhamma through their own lives. Within any other religion, can they make the same claim No, they cannot say, "come and see". They would have to say, "come and believe". This Dhamma is to come and see, come and understand, and come and realize.

The fifth quality is *opanayika*. *Opanayika* means that this Dhamma is to be *experienced through one's own life*. It is because this Dhamma is about our own eyes, our own ears, our own nose, our own tongue, our own body and our own mind.

The sixth quality is *paccattam veditabbo viññūhīti*. That means that this Dhamma is *for the wise to understand, individually* – through their own effort.

These are the great qualities of the Dhamma. Because of these qualities, we can develop an unshakeable confidence in the Dhamma.

Developing an Unshakeable Confidence in the Sangha

The third factor of a Stream Entrant is an unshakeable confidence in the Sangha. We must recognize the great qualities of the followers of the Supreme Buddha. These are the Noble Disciples who are trying to achieve happiness in this very life and are trying to develop their wisdom.

The first quality of the Sangha is *supatipanna*. *Supatipanna* means that they follow the path to eradicate passion, lust, ill-will, hatred, and delusion. This is the first quality of the Supreme Buddha's followers. The *Arahant* quality meant that our Great Teacher eradicated lust towards forms, towards sounds, towards odours, towards tastes, towards tangibles, and towards mind-objects. The followers are also trying to do the same. That is called *supatipanna*. One must recognize that this is the only community who is trying to eradicate lust towards forms, sounds, odours, tastes, tangibles and mind-objects, and they are following the Noble Eightfold Path to achieve this goal.

The second quality is *ujupatipanno*. *Uju* means '*the straight way*'. The Sangha is following the straight way, which is the Noble Eightfold Path. In this world, the Sangha is the only community who follows the straight way. The Path leading to the cessation of suffering is one of the Four Noble Truths. They are trying to follow the Noble Eightfold Path with: Right View, Right Intention, Right Speech, Right Action, Right Livelihood, Right Effort, Right Mindfulness and Right Concentration. Those that follow this Path are called the *followers of the Supreme Buddha*.

The third quality is *ñāyapatipanno*. *Ñāyapatipanno* means that the Sangha is following the Path to understand the Four Noble Truths. The Teacher is the one who understood the Four Noble Truths, and the followers are also trying to understand the Four Noble Truths.

The fourth quality is *sāmīcipatipanno*. *Sāmīcipatipanno* means the followers of the Supreme Buddha *teach the Dhamma to others*. And, followers who hold all these qualities, are worthy of receiving offerings and reverence. These are the great qualities of the Sangha. Because of these qualities, we can develop an unshakeable confidence in the Sangha.

Developing Moral Discipline

The fourth factor of a Stream Entrant is observance of **the Five Precepts**. These are:

• abstaining from killing beings,
• abstaining from taking that which is not given (stealing),
• abstaining from sexual misconduct,
• abstaining from false speech, and
• abstaining from taking intoxicating drinks and drugs.

True Love and Compassion

Supreme Buddha advises that if one has love and compassion for another (for example, for one's parents, relatives and friends), then one should teach them the factors of a Stream Entrant. These factors are:

1. an unshakeable confidence in the Buddha,
2. an unshakeable confidence in the Dhamma,
3. an unshakeable confidence in the Sangha, and
4. following the Five Precepts in an unbreakable way.

If someone has achieved these factors, then after this life, they will avoid being born in a bad destination (in hell, animal and ghost worlds), and can reach the ultimate liberation of *Nibbāna* within a maximum of seven births. This is the *real assurance* to life, and it all begins with having noble friends.

Sādhu! Sādhu! Sādhu!

May you have the opportunity to understand the Four Noble Truths in Gautama Sammā Sambuddha's Dispensation.

⌘ Mahānāma Sutta
The Householder's Path to Nibbāna

ANGUTTARA NIKĀYA 6:10

Dear friends, today we are going to discuss the Mahānāma Sutta from the Anguttara Nikāya. The Buddha expounded this discourse when he visited the Sakyan capital of Kapilavatthu. There, the Sakyan Chief Mahānāma, approached the Enlightened One and invited him to stay in a hermitage called the Nigrodha Monastery.

One day, Mahānāma visited the Enlightened One and having venerated Him, asked the following question: "Blessed One, the noble disciple (*ariya sāvaka*) who has fully understood the Teachings of the Buddha and attained its fruits, with what thoughts does he frequently abide?"

Recollecting the Great Qualities of Supreme Buddha

The Buddha replied, "Mahānāma, the noble disciple who has understood the dispensation of the Teacher and has entered the path to liberation, abides recollecting the supreme qualities of the Tathāgatha (the Enlightened One) in this way:

'The Blessed One is accomplished *(araham)*; fully enlightened *(sammā sambuddho)*; perfect in true knowledge and conduct *(vijjācaranasampanno)*; sublime *(sugato)*; the knower of all worlds *(lokavidu)*; incomparable leader of persons to be tamed *(anuttaro purisa dammasarathi)*; teacher of devas and humans *(satthā devamanussānam)*; enlightened *(Buddho)* and blessed *(bhagavā)*.'

Refuge is not based upon one's own intelligence, but on the wisdom and the qualities of a supreme being who was self-enlightened, and therefore, is incomparable. One who recognizes the exceptional qualities and the greatness of the Blessed One takes refuge in **the Triple Gem – the Buddha** (the Enlightened One), **the Dhamma** (the Doctrine) and **the Sangha** (the community of disciples of the Buddha). He takes refuge in the Triple Gem with a complete understanding of the great qualities of each Gem.

The Buddha said, "Mahānāma, when the noble disciple recollects the qualities of the Tathāgatha, his mind is not afflicted with sensual desire *(rāga)*, with hatred *(dosa)*, or with delusion *(moha)*. His mind becomes steadfast and unshaken towards the Teacher. When he has perfect confidence in the Tathāgatha, he gains inspiration in the true meaning of the Dhamma. He gains gladness connected with the Dhamma. When he is glad, rapture and joy are born in him. When he is joyous, his body becomes tranquil. One whose body is tranquil, feels pleasure. When he experiences pleasure, his mind becomes concentrated."

"He abides calm among people holding conflicting views. He abides untroubled among distressed people. He enters the Path of the Dhamma. He abides recollecting the supreme qualities of the Buddha."

These benefits are possible if one is mindful, because then, there is no delusion. We too can obtain these benefits by being mindful and taking refuge in the Triple Gem.

The Four Noble Truths

The noble disciple also recollects the supreme qualities of the Dhamma (or the Doctrine expounded by the Enlightened One). *Svākkhato bhagavatā Dhammo* means 'this Dhamma has been well proclaimed by the Enlightened One'. To reflect on the Dhamma, one must have a good knowledge of it. If one has not learned the Dhamma, one would not know that the Dhamma has been well explained, and is therefore capable of being misled by various other theories one hears. Contemporary man tries to hold up the Dhamma against modern psychology to see if they are compatible. There is a stanza in the Ratana Sutta – the Jewels Discourse, explained by the Buddha:

Khayam virāgam amatam panītam
Yad ajjhagā Sakyamunī samāhito
Na tena Dhammena samatthi kiñci

"There is nothing in the world that can be compared to the Dhamma proclaimed by the Sakyan Sage, which destroys all defilements and leads to the deathless state of Nibbāna."

The Buddha's Doctrine is the Four Noble Truths. A Buddha appears in the world to make known and explain the Four Noble Truths. If one talks about the Dhamma of the Enlightened One, it is the Four Noble Truths that one would describe. The Buddha first explained the Noble Truth that should be fully understood. This is the **Noble Truth of Suffering** – *Dukkham Ariya Saccam*. The *Pāli* word *dukkha* covers a range of meanings. It incorporates suffering (both mental and physical), dissatisfaction, unpleasantness, and others. The Noble Truth that should be eradicated is the *Noble Truth of the Origin of Suffering – Dukkha Samudayam Ariya Saccam*. The Noble Truth that should be realized is the *Noble Truth of the Cessation of Suffering – Dukkha Nirodham Ariya Saccam*. The Noble Truth that should be followed is the *Noble Truth of the Path leading to the Cessation of Suffering, the Noble Eightfold Path – Dukkha Nirodha Gāminī Patipadā Ariya Saccam*. The validity of these Truths does not change with time, and therefore they are called *Noble Truths*.

The Buddha explained that birth is painful, problematic, and unsatisfactory; aging is unpleasant; illness is suffering; death is unpleasant and is suffering; association with the disliked and separation from loved ones are unpleasant; and not getting what one wants causes grief. In this context, not getting what one wants does not mean the ordinary day to day things we like to have. Not getting what one wants is the dissatisfaction that comes from unavoidable forms of suffering encountered in life. Beings, subject to ill health and sickness, wish to be free of these, but this does not always happen. That is *dissatisfaction*. No one likes to grow old or die. No one wishes to be parted from loved ones or to associate with those who are unpleasant. Those who understand the unsatisfactory nature of life do not want to face the danger of another birth, and wish not to be born again. However, this cannot be achieved by mere wishing.

Dukkha cannot be understood merely by experiencing suffering. Supreme Buddha, before his enlightenment, while he was still seeking the truth, practised severe austerities, giving unbearable pain and suffering to the body. If the truth of suffering could be penetrated and understood by mere suffering, he would have become enlightened at that time. But Supreme Buddha gave up that approach, as it failed to produce effective results.

It is through the Noble Eightfold Path that a complete understanding of this suffering (*dukkha*) is possible, and ultimately guides one to the cessation of suffering. The Enlightened One has given us a method to achieve the cessation of suffering, a Doctrine – one that is clear, with correct meaning, well explained, perfect, and pure. In this Doctrine the Buddha has shown the cause of suffering to be craving *(tanhā)*, and that craving brings about a fresh birth *(ponobhavikā)*. It conditions another existence. Everyone has craving inherent in him or her, and it is not easy to eradicate. But unless it is overcome, a renewal of existence is a certainty. If we get killed suddenly in a road accident, there will be an immediate birth somewhere. This is because we have not abandoned craving. Once there is a birth, there arises dissatisfaction, sorrow, lamentation, pain, grief and despair – the whole mass of suffering.

Sometimes, when we are disenchanted with life, we say death would end all of our troubles, but this does not happen. In fact, *troubles* then become two-fold – with death and an immediate birth. Suffering incorporates a phenomenon by which the cause, *(tanhā)* craving or desire, always conditions an effect. The effect is another existence. It was this way in the past, it is the same today, and will be the same in the future. This same law will always be in effect, and therefore, the cause for suffering is a Noble Truth.

In This Very Life

In the time of the future Maitriya Buddha, this same Doctrine will be heard, seen and practised. Before the Maitriya Buddha appears, life in this world system will come to near extinction. Then, with evolution, life spans will again reach more than a hundred thousand years before gradually declining again. This is what the Supreme Buddha has told us will happen. As ordinary beings or uninstructed persons, there is no certainty to when and where one will exist. If by some chance, a heinous crime *(ānantariya pāpa kamma)* is committed, and the inevitable period in hell has been paid by the doer of that crime, the current *Buddha Sāsana* (dispensation) may have ended by then. This is how we have travelled the repeated cycle of birth and death *(samsāra)*. There is no one who has not had a birth in hell, the ghost world, and the animal world. In between those unfortunate births, due to some great fortune and the merit of wholesome actions, we now have a human life. However, the danger of descending to the lower realms in a future birth is still very possible. The only way to escape this danger is to develop beyond an ordinary being, and enter the path to liberation *(Sotāpanna – Stream Entrant stage)* while still in this human life, and while we can hear and learn the Noble Teachings of the Supreme Buddha.

To achieve this, complete understanding and penetration of the Four Noble Truths in this very life are essential. *Craving* is present because of ignorance, delusion and a lack of understanding. There is craving for sensual pleasures, craving for existence, and craving for non-existence. If there is even a remnant of any of these cravings, the cycle of birth and death continues with no end. This means the continuation of unsatisfactory states of being. If we develop true understanding, knowledge and vision of reality, we will not maintain any craving within ourselves. We will realize that it is a result of delusion, and eradicate craving completely. It is something that can be eradicated, and the method to do so is found in the Noble Eightfold Path.

One who realizes the unsatisfactory nature of this life will try to find its cause. Through the Doctrine of the Supreme Buddha, one understands that the cause for suffering is desire and craving. He accepts the teaching that one can overcome this suffering, and investigates the method to achieve this. He then finds the Noble Eightfold Path, which is the practical course of action expounded by the Supreme Buddha, to achieve the end of suffering.

The Noble Eightfold Path is:

- **Right Understanding or Right View** (*Sammā Ditthi*) – which is the knowledge of the Four Noble Truths.

- **Right Intention** (*Sammā Sankappa*) – which is directing the mind towards understanding and fully realizing the Four Noble Truths.

- **Right Speech** (*Sammā Vācā*) – which is abstaining from false, harsh and malicious speech, and indulging only in speech that is conducive to right understanding.

- **Right Action** (*Sammā Kammanta*) – which is abstaining from wrong bodily action and acting for the benefit of oneself and others.

- **Right Livelihood** (*Sammā Ājīva*) – which is abstaining from defiled actions, and leading a blameless occupation.

- **Right Effort** (*Sammā Vāyāma*) – which is effort directed towards overcoming defilements and unwholesomeness, and cultivating and maintaining wholesomeness.

- **Right Mindfulness** (*Sammā Sati*) – which is developing the four foundations of mindfulness (mindfulness in contemplating the body, mindfulness in contemplating feelings, mindfulness in contemplating the mind, and mindfulness in contemplating mind-objects).

- **Right Concentration** (*Sammā Samādhi*) – which is developing the concentration of mind, associated with wholesomeness and attained through meditation.

This is the Path leading to the realization of *Nibbāna*, and should be understood well by the noble disciple. One who becomes proficient in this Path will undoubtedly end all suffering. This is a Noble Truth.

Recollecting the Great Qualities of the Dhamma

The Buddha explains next that the noble disciple who is skilled in the Enlightened One's Dhamma, recollects that the Dhamma or the Doctrine, has been well proclaimed *(svākkhāto bhagavatā dhammo)*. The Dhamma is excellent in the beginning, excellent in the middle, and excellent in the end. There is no confusion, and it is perfect and pure. He establishes his confidence in the Dhamma. Skilled in the Dhamma, he recollects with confidence that the Dhamma, when practised diligently, gives results in this lifetime itself *(sanditthiko)*. Having accepted that the Supreme Buddha's Dhamma has been well proclaimed, he recollects with confidence that it is indeed a *true* Dhamma, which does not change with time and is equally relevant in the past, present and the future *(akāliko)*. He recollects with faith that the Dhamma, which invites everyone to 'come and see' *(ehipassiko)*, should be investigated. He understands that the Dhamma should be examined by himself, and its benefits seen within oneself *(opaniko)*.

The noble disciple understands that if he accepts this Dhamma (which has been well explained, is visible in this very life, does not change with time, and its benefits seen within him) then, according to the wisdom he has developed, he can attain the fruits of a *Sotāpanna* (a Stream Entrant), a *Sakadāgāmi* (a Once-Returner), an *Anāgāmi* (a Non-Returner), and an *Arahant* (a fully

Accomplished One). This Dhamma is to be realized by the wise, not by the unwise.

When the noble disciple understands and recollects the Dhamma wisely, he becomes established in the truth. As he continues recollecting, joy arises in him. His mind becomes free of greed, hatred and delusion. The Buddha explains that with joy in his mind, his body becomes tranquil, and happiness arises in him. He becomes peaceful. In a turbulent world, he abides calm and untroubled. We too, can gain all of these benefits by wisely reflecting on the supreme qualities of the Supreme Buddha's Dhamma.

Recollecting the Great Qualities of the Sangha

Next, the Supreme Buddha explains that the noble disciple who has understood the dispensation of the Blessed One, and has entered the path to liberation, abides recollecting the supreme qualities of the Sangha, the Buddha's community of disciples who practise the Doctrine. The word *Sangha* means *'a community'*. This community is comprised of the Noble Disciples *(Āriya Sangha)*, led by the Arahant Sāriputta and Arahant Moggallāna, who were the chief disciples of the Buddha. The Sangha includes: the fully Accomplished Ones, the Non-Returners, the Once-Returners, and the Stream Entrants who have entered the Path. This community of Sangha existed in the Buddha's time, exists now, and will exist in the future.

The noble disciple knows that these states (or fruits of the Path) can be attained if the Dhamma is well practised. He recollects the supreme qualities of the Sangha. He recollects that the Blessed One's disciples practise to rid themselves of greed, hatred and delusion *(supatipanno)*; they follow a straight and direct Path, which is the Noble Eightfold Path *(ujupatipanno)*; they follow a practice which leads them to a full understanding of the Four Noble Truths (ñāyapatipanno); and they spread the Supreme Buddha's Dhamma and its method of practice to the entire world (sāmīcīpatipanno). The community of Sangha, following this path to liberation, is worthy of gifts brought from near and far. They are worthy of hospitality. They are worthy of offerings for the gaining of merit. They are worthy of respect and worship. This community is an incomparable field of goodness for the world.

As with recollecting the great qualities of the Buddha and the Dhamma, when the noble disciple recollects the qualities of the Sangha, he becomes established in the Truth. As he continues recollecting, joy arises in him. His mind becomes free of greed, hatred and delusion. The Buddha explains that with joy in his mind, his body becomes tranquil, and happiness arises in him. He becomes peaceful. In a turbulent world, he abides calm and untroubled. We too, can gain all of these benefits by developing wise reflection on the supreme qualities of the Buddha, Dhamma and Sangha.

The Responsibility is with You

During the time of the Buddha, the lay disciple, Suppavāsā, had very agonizing labour pains due to a delayed childbirth. She practised recollecting the qualities of the Buddha to ease her pain. Upon hearing this from Suppavāsā's husband, the Supreme Buddha blessed the mother and the child, and a healthy baby boy was born. This boy later entered the Order and became Arahant Sīvalī. To celebrate the joy of having a son, the parents wanted to offer alms to the Buddha and the Sangha for seven days. As the Arahant Moggallana had already accepted another invitation on behalf of the Buddha, he went to the first lay supporter to request a change of date. The supporter was willing if the Arahant Moggallana could guarantee that the raw material he had already purchased for the alms offering would not perish, and his faith in the Triple Gem would not change. The Arahant replied that he could use his well developed spiritual powers to prevent the raw material from perishing, but as to the supporter's faith, the Arahant could do nothing. The supporter himself was responsible to ensure that his faith was well established. This story demonstrates that *unshakeable confidence* and faith is the sole responsibility of the individual.

Once when Arahant Pilindavaccha was walking, he saw a little girl sobbing while she stood beside her very poor mother. The mother said that a salesman had gone by, but she did not have any money to buy her daughter a gold chain. The Arahant picked up a piece of string from the road, tied the ends together and asked the woman to put it around the little girl's neck. It immediately became a shining gold necklace. The girl showed off her possession and the people around were suspicious of how she obtained it. They reported the suspicion to the king who imprisoned the whole family. The next day, the Arahant, finding the house closed, learned of what happened and visited the king. The king explained the reasons for arresting the family. To demonstrate what had actually happened, the Arahant asked the king to look round the pillars of his palace, which had turned to gem-studded gold. The king realized the error and not only released the family, but also offered a whole village in the name of the Arahant to his supporters. This is the first recorded model village in the world, and the king was King Bimbisara.

These stories illustrate the supreme qualities and powers of the Sangha and when one reflects on these and many others with faith, one is filled with wonderment and admiration for the lives of the great Arahants like Sāriputta, Moggallana and Pilindavaccha. The noble disciple establishes himself in faith by recollecting these qualities of the Sangha.

Recollecting One's Own Virtue

Next, the Supreme Buddha advises the noble disciple to recollect qualities of his own virtue and morality *(sīla)*, which is the conscious and intentional restraint from unwholesome bodily and verbal actions. The Exalted One has shown that purity of *sīla*, or a high moral standard, is helpful in gaining concentration *(samādhi)*.

The noble disciple establishes himself in the Five Precepts, and if he falters and there is a lapse, he immediately re-establishes himself in the precepts. He understands and respects the value of morality. He abstains from killing, abstains from taking what is not given, abstains from sexual misconduct, abstains from wrong speech, and abstains from taking intoxicants. These precepts must be guarded with great care, and not half-heartedly with allowance for infringements. In addition, Buddhists observe the full-moon day as a day of fasting when meals are not taken after midday. On that day, they abstain from sensual pleasures and the use of high and luxurious seats and beds. Time is entirely dedicated to the practice of the Dhamma. This observance of the Eight Precepts should be practised regularly as a development of inner strength.

Recollecting One's Own Generosity

The Enlightened One's disciple is one who values the giving of alms *(dāna)*. The Buddha emphasized that greed and stinginess should be abandoned. This defilement also incorporates jealousy. If one shares what he has with others, he eliminates stinginess and develops generosity *(cāga)*. Helping others and seeing others happy in their gains, helps to eliminate jealousy. Greed is very dangerous and can give birth in animal realms. The noble disciple understands these dangers, develops the art of giving and kindness, and thereby practises detachment. He can gain the benefits of pure thoughts by wisely reflecting on his own good deeds of generosity.

Recollecting the Qualities of Heavenly Beings

The Buddha explained how the noble disciple reflects on *devas* or heavenly beings. Having listened to the Blessed One's Teachings, the noble disciple knows that there are heavenly beings in the higher realms. He recollects that these beings are born in divine abodes due to their faith in the Triple Gem, their virtue, their generosity, their knowledge of the Dhamma, and their wisdom; developed while in the human world. He reflects that he too is developing these same practices, and therefore has these divine qualities. He is confident that he too can be born in these heavenly realms.

Ultimate Liberation Attained by Recollecting Great Qualities

The Supreme Buddha explained that disciples who lead a householder's life can realize *Nibbāna* by following this practice intelligently. By recollecting the supreme qualities of the Buddha, Dhamma and Sangha; recollecting the benefits of morality; recollecting acts of generosity; and recollecting the qualities of heavenly beings, he could be born in the heavenly abodes as a *devatā*, who is on the path to *Nibbāna*.

Such a person having lived in the Doctrine of the Enlightened One, although born in the heavens, does not get attached to divine pleasures. He continues his practice of the Dhamma, and even more ardently, continues reflecting on the qualities of the Buddha, Dhamma and Sangha. Thereafter, by continuing these practices in the heavenly abodes, he could realize *Nibbāna*, the ultimate liberation from suffering.

Birth as a human being is a rare occurrence. Therefore, it must be appreciated that this is a rare opportunity to learn and understand the Dhamma. The six recollections explained by the fully enlightened Buddha should be practised and developed without delay. One who cultivates this practice will have a clear, untroubled mind at the time of death, thereby gaining birth in a happy existence, from where he could realize the ultimate deliverance, *Nibbāna*.

Sādhu! Sādhu! Sādhu!

May you have the opportunity to understand the Four Noble Truths in Gautama Sammā Sambuddha's Dispensation.

ଔ *Mahādukkhakkhandha Sutta* *Beyond Gratification*

MAJJHIMA NIKĀYA 13

*V*enerable Mahā Sangha and meritorious followers, today we are going to learn a very important discourse from the Majjhima Nikāya (Middle Length Discourses). The name of this discourse is Mahādukkhakkhandha Sutta – the Greater Discourse on the Mass of Suffering.

Through our discussions and listening to discourses, we have come to understand the fundamental purpose of the Teachings of the Buddha. The purpose is to overcome *dukkha* (suffering). To overcome dukkha, the disciples must understand the Four Noble Truths. The main purpose of the appearance of the Buddha, is to teach the Four Noble Truths.

The Noble Truth of Suffering

The first truth is The Noble Truth of Suffering - *Dukkha*. Can you remember what should be done with suffering as a Noble Truth? The Noble Truth of Suffering must be *understood*. Understanding means, we need to learn about suffering, and then we must investigate suffering in our own lives through wise consideration *(yonisomanasikāra)*. If we can develop wise consideration to understand and realize suffering, then gradually we will be able to understand the way to eradicate the origin of suffering. As Buddha explained, in our life there is always an arranging of suffering. What is the reason for this suffering? The reason is ignorance. What's the meaning of ignorance? The meaning of ignorance is *not knowing the Four Noble Truths* – not knowing suffering, not knowing the origin of suffering, not knowing the cessation of suffering, and not knowing the path leading to the cessation of suffering. The arranging of suffering, is always active in our lives. The most important thing for us to do is to try and understand suffering. Then we will be able to understand the origin of suffering in our own lives.

Distorted Vision

Because of the ignorance present in our lives, there is a certain kind of vision. According to Buddha's Teachings, this vision is called *'distorted vision'*. In other words, when we perceive the external world as noble disciples we must recognize that we struggle with the external world due to this ignorance and distorted vision.

What is meant by *'external world'*? Buddha explained the world as it refers to one's eye, ear, nose, tongue, body and mind. The external world means: the world of eye (forms cognizable by the eye), the world of ear (sounds cognizable by the ear), the world of nose (odours cognizable by the nose), the world of tongue (flavours cognizable by the tongue), the world of body (tangibles cognizable by the body), and the world of mind (thoughts or mental objects cognizable by the mind). This is the external world that we perceive in a distorted manner.

In the Anguttara Nikāya, the Numerical Discourses of the Buddha, our Great Teacher describes in detail this *distorted perception (saññā vipallāsa)*:

* *anicche nicca saññā* – one perceives the impermanent things as permanent,
* *dukkhe sukha saññā* – one perceives unpleasant things as pleasant,
* *asubhe subha saññā* – one perceives that which is ugly as beautiful, and
* *anatte attha saññā* – one perceives things without self as self.

We perceive things in this way, because of ignorance. Supreme Buddha then explained, that because of this ignorance there will be the arranging of suffering or the cycle of births and deaths *(samsāra)*.

Supreme Buddha tried to explain these realities in different ways to his disciples – with great compassion, and using many similes and stories. Buddha states in one simile: *"avijjā nīvaranānam sathānam tanhā sanyojana"*, which means *"hindered by ignorance, fettered by craving"*. Because of distorted perception, that exists as a result of ignorance and delusion, there will be craving.

However, if we could clearly understand impermanence, what would be the result? We would not cling to impermanent things. We would understand in this way: *'if I were to cling to these things, then because of their impermanent nature, I will have to suffer'*. With this understanding, one would try hard not to be attached to these things.

In reality, however, the nature of the mind is ready to cling to impermanent things. We build our world around impermanent things, and we develop craving for them. We are unable to understand the reality and impurity of things, so we cling to them.

When we can't understand things as they really are (that is, *without self*), we try to control them: *'This should be like this. This should not be like this.'* We imagine things the way we think they should be, and then try to control them. When it is time to face reality, we will have to suffer. Yet, what is the real nature of things? Yes, they are all without *self* and are imperment. It is a doctrine or phenomenon.

We must understand what is meant by the concept of being 'hindered by ignorance'. What does 'hindered' mean? It means *'covered by a hard shell'*. We are inside a shell, and it is difficult to break that shell of ignorance, as the shell is very hard. As a noble disciple of the Buddha, we must also understand craving. What is *craving*? It is a fetter – a chain or bond, or restraint; like shackles. Supreme Buddha explains that because of this nature, *'hindered by ignorance, fettered by craving'*, we have been travelling in countless cycles of birth and death.

Buddha uses another simile to elaborate and explain. Let's take the example of a small stick. If someone were to throw a stick into the sky, when the stick falls to the earth, it may land on its side. Another time, it may land on one end. Another time, the stick may land on the other end, etc. Like the stick, Buddha explains, on one occasion, someone can be born in the human world, and on another occasion, in hell, in the ghost world, or in the animal world. This is the danger of *saṃsāra*. The reason for this is because we are hindered by ignorance, fettered by craving.

The Buddha states, *"Now, it is enough. It is enough to understand this mass of suffering; enough to be liberated from this mass of suffering".* (SN 15) Buddha explains very clearly the nature of suffering. If one wants to understand suffering, he can do so through Buddha's Teachings. In this discourse we can learn a lot of things about the arranging of suffering and how to escape from suffering. The most important thing to realize is that in Buddha's Teachings, one can find the origin of suffering and also the end of suffering. There is the dark side, *and* the bright side. First, Buddha explains the dark side, and then Buddha explains the bright side. Listen carefully and develop your own wise consideration about these realities of life.

The Discourse

The Blessed One was living in Sāvatthi, Jetta's Grove, Anathapindika's Park. As our Great Teacher often lived in Anathapindika's Park, many of the discourses were delivered there. In the morning, a number of monks were preparing to go on their alms round. After dressing and taking their bowls, they went to Sāvatthi for alms in the morning. On the way, they felt it was too early for alms, so they went to a park where recluses of different religions had gathered.

In the park, the monks of Buddha's Order exchanged greetings with the other recluses, and sat down to one side. While waiting, the other recluses asked of Buddha's Noble Disciples the following question: *"Friends, the recluse Gautama (samana Gautama) describes the full understanding of sensual pleasures. And, so do we. Recluse Gautama describes the full understanding of material form. And, so do we. Recluse Gautama describes the full understanding of feeling. And, so do we. In that case, what is the difference; what is the distinction or the variance, between the recluse Gautama's teaching and ours?"*

Do you know why these recluses call the Supreme Buddha *'recluse Gautama'*? It is because those recluses of other religions did not have reverence and respect for the Buddha. That is why they called the Buddha, 'recluse (or *samana)* Gautama'.

In the beginning we discussed that suffering should be understood. We discussed sensual pleasures when we discussed our dealings with the outer world. We spoke about our desire for forms, sounds, odours, flavours, tangibles and thoughts. What is the meaning of the Five Aggregates of Clinging *(sankhittena pañcupādānakandā dukkhā)*? When Buddha explains the Noble Truth of Suffering, at the end of that explanation, Buddha teaches that the *Five Aggregates of Clinging* are suffering. Can you remember the Five Aggregates of Clinging? They are:

* *material form (rūpa)* aggregate of clinging,
* *feeling (vedanā)* aggregate of clinging,
* *perception (saññā)* aggregate of clinging,
* *formation (sankhāra)* aggregate of clinging, and
* *consciousness (viññāna)* aggregate of clinging.

So here, the question from the recluses, makes reference to the aggregates of material form and feeling (from the Five Aggregates of Clinging).

Going back to the question asked of the Buddha's Disciples, the other recluses claimed that their teachers preached the same doctrine as the Buddha. They then asked about the difference in the teachings. Buddha's Disciples were not able to respond to this question. Without approving or disapproving Buddha's Disciples rose from their seats, departed, and thought to go and ask this question of the Blessed One. Why did the monks think to go and ask the Supreme Buddha? Yes, it is because the monks know that they are the followers of the Blessed One, and the Blessed One is *the Teacher*.

We have come to the most important part, but before we discuss Buddha's answer, I would like to give you an example to help you understand. Let's consider 'a cake' for our example. Do you bake cakes? If you were to say that you understand and know about cakes, what would be the meaning of this statement? The meaning would be that you know how to prepare a cake, the ingredients used, the process of baking, etc. Further, you would be familiar with the taste. You would also be aware of the drawbacks, or the dangers of eating cake – high fat, sugar, etc. So if we say that 'we know about cakes', it means that we understand cakes in this way – completely.

Buddha explains we must understand things in three ways:

• The first way is to understand the *gratification (assāda)*.
• The second way is to understand the *danger (ādīnava)*.
• The third way is to understand the *escape (nissarana)*.

After paying homage to the Buddha the disciples told the Buddha what had happened and the question that was asked of them. Buddha explained to his monks that when other recluses question the Buddha's Disciples in this way, the recluses themselves, should be questioned in this manner: *"Friends, what is the gratification; what is the danger; and what is the escape of sensual pleasure?"*

They should be questioned: *"Friends, what is the gratification; what is the danger; and what is the escape of material forms?"*

They should be questioned: *"Friends, what is the gratification, what is the danger, and what is the escape of feeling?*

If they were to be questioned in this manner, the recluses from other religions would not be able to answer. Why? These other recluses do not understand sensual pleasure, material form and feeling in the three ways that they should be understood. Buddha explains that no one else in the world, among Māras, Brahmas and recluses can answer this question except for a Buddha or one of Buddha's Noble Disciples.

Keep these three words in your mind: *assāda* means *'gratification'*; *ādīnava* means *'danger'*, and *nissarana* means *'escape'*. These are three key words in Buddha's Teachings. We will discuss these in detail.

Assāda - Gratification (in the case of Sensual Pleasures)

Buddha explained in detail 'gratification' in the case of sensual pleasure. Firstly, there are **five chords of sensual pleasures**. They are:

- forms cognizable by the eye that are wished for, desired, agreeable and likeable,
- sounds cognizable by the ear that are wished for, desired, agreeable and likeable,
- odours cognizable by the nose that are wished for, desired, agreeable and likeable,
- flavours cognizable by the tongue that are wished for, desired, agreeable and likeable, and
- tangibles cognizable by the body that are wished for, desired, agreeable and likeable.

Now let's try to understand the sensual pleasure in material forms. Here, the meaning of sensual pleasure is: when we see a form, in that form there is a nature that *gives pleasure and enjoyment* to the mind. When we perceive that form, there is pleasure.

Sensual pleasure in sounds is the *pleasurable nature* in sounds that arouses joy and gratification in the mind. We enjoy ourselves with these sounds and are eager to listen to them over and over again.

Sensual pleasure in odours is the *pleasurable nature* in an odour that arouses joy and gratification in the mind. The odour is agreeable, wished for and desired. We find ourselves seeking this odour – *'Where is that nice smell coming from?'*

Sensual pleasure in flavours is the *pleasurable nature* in a flavour that arouses joy and gratification in the mind. The flavour is agreeable, wished for and desired.

Sensual pleasure in tangibles is the *pleasurable nature* in a tangible that arouses joy and gratification in the mind. The tangible is agreeable, wished for and desired. For instance, when we look for a cushion to sit on, we check to make sure that it is comfortable.

We can relate to these things, can't we? It is because we are always trying to find satisfaction through sensual pleasures. Buddha explains that though there are the five chords of sensual pleasures, the *gratification* which arises out of sensual pleasure is something different.

Buddha explains *'gratification'* in the case of sensual pleasures. What is the meaning of gratification? The pleasure *(sukham)* and joy *(somanassam)* that arise *dependent* on the five chords of sensual pleasure is the *'gratification in the case of sensual pleasures'*.

Let's take these flowers as an example. There is gratification, is there not? We think, *'Oh they look very beautiful, and they smell beautiful'*. But in reality, within a few days, they will die. You won't be able to see the flowers dying since we remove and discard them when they begin to wilt. What are we doing here when we remove them? We are hiding the reality and only showing the gratification to the world. This is done throughout television, advertisement posters, newspapers and radio. This is the nature of the world of ordinary beings. They propagate gratification and they hide the danger and the dissatisfaction. That's why it is very hard to understand suffering without wise consideration.

Ādīnava – Danger (in the case of Sensual Pleasures)

Buddha explains the danger in the case of sensual pleasures. A man or woman must earn money to live. To earn money, he or she must work. To work, one must face the elements of cold and heat. Here, in Canada, during winter it is very cold. A few months ago, you wore jackets to protect yourselves from the cold. These days it is very hot, so we turn to air-conditioning to cool ourselves from the heat. One is injured by the contact of mosquitoes and the sun, and one experiences the risk of hunger and thirst. One is always experiencing loss, yet one still has to work to earn money. Buddha explains that this is one of the dangers in the case of sensual pleasures. Though there is gratification (jobs allow us to earn money to eat well, to look after our sons and daughters, to pay the mortgage, for entertainment and to enjoy life), Buddha explains that compared to the little gratification, the dangers are great.

By working, one strives and puts forth effort to earn money. However, if one does not own any property, for example, one can think that there is no fruitful outcome. He will lament with sorrow and weep, beating his hands to his chest and ask, *'Oh, what has happened to me? My effort is fruitless and my work has been in vain!'* This is the danger in the case of sensual pleasure. Isn't this the case in our lives? Yes, we also try to achieve gratification, but the results are not always what we desire.

Then Buddha explains that if property is obtained and his efforts are successful, there comes another problem. What is that problem? Yes, he has to protect his wealth and he experiences pain and grief in trying to protect it. Why? He worries, *'Will the government take my wealth through taxes? Will thieves come and steal this money? Will water sweep it away? Will fire burn it?'* Always, in his mind, there will be the problem of how to protect his wealth. It is easy for us to relate to this, isn't it? We have to understand this fear as a danger of sensual pleasures. We are always trying to protect our property. Though one tries to protect these things, after some kind of loss, he then thinks, *'What I once had, I have no longer.'* He feels sorrow, grieves, laments and regrets. This grief is another danger in the case of sensual pleasures.

Buddha explains further. With sensual pleasures as the cause, ministers and rulers quarrel with each other; householders quarrel with each other; mothers quarrel with sons; sons quarrel with mothers; sons quarrel with fathers; brothers quarrel with sisters. What is the reason? They quarrel with each other because of sensual pleasures. They quarrel over things like inheritance. It is because of greed and the craving to enjoy with sensual pleasures. Isn't that right?

All the problems throughout the world are because of sensual pleasure. Buddha explains disputes arise, and people attack each other with harsh words, sticks and knives. And ultimately, suffering and even death can result. People fight over the ownership of land with weapons, bombs, etc. People break into homes and commit burglary. Then, the police will catch these wrongdoers and they will have to face suffering in the form of punishment by going to jail. This is another danger in the case of sensual pleasure.

All of this is the *'mass of suffering'* as a result of sensual pleasure. All these things can be seen, here and now, in this very life. As a result of the struggle to find gratification through sensual pleasures, one will indulge in misconduct of body, speech, and mind. That means killing others, stealing, indulging in sexual misconduct, speaking harshly, speaking maliciously, lying, having an unwholesome and covetous mind, and acting with ill will and jealousy. As a result of having indulged in misconduct through body, speech and mind, after the dissolution of the body, he will be born in a bad destination. The mass of suffering will be the result in the next life that follows as well.

After explaining the gratification of sensual pleasures and the dangers of sensual pleasures, Supreme Buddha explains next *the escape of sensual pleasures*.

Nissarana - Escape (in the case of Sensual Pleasures)

Buddha explains that escape *(nissarana)* is *"yo chandarāga pahānāya"*. That means if someone can *remove the desire or the lust towards sensual pleasures, he or she would escape from sensual pleasures*. So, what is meant here by removal? We need to remove the craving and lust towards desirable forms, desirable sounds, desirable odours, desirable tastes and desirable tangibles. If someone wants to remove lust and craving for forms, sounds, odours, flavours and tangibles, then that person must understand that these are the things that bring suffering to one's life. First, he needs to realize that fact. An ordinary person will not be able to understand this as he will want to enjoy his life with the very same things. A noble disciple must understand as Buddha understood, and as Buddha has taught us.

Gratification in the case of Material Form

What is the gratification in the case of material form? Do you know what is meant by *'material form'*? Material forms *(rūpa)* are all things derived by the four great elements. That means, all things derived by: the earth element, the water element, the air element and the fire element. In this discourse, the Buddha explains this in a very interesting way by asking a question.

Buddha asks the disciples, *"Suppose there was a girl in her fifteenth or sixteenth year, neither too tall, nor too short; neither too thin, nor too fat; neither too dark, nor too fair. What do you think monks, is she beautiful and lovely?"* (Remember that in Buddha's time, girls were at a marriageable age around fifteen or sixteen years old.)

The monks replied, *"Yes, Venerable Sir, she is very beautiful."*

Buddha then states, *"The pleasure and joy that arise dependent on that beauty and loveliness is the gratification in the case of material form."*

When we listen to these discourses, do you think that it is difficult to follow and understand the Dhamma? Are we able to understand it? Yes, we can understand. For example, when we look at these flowers, they are beautiful flowers and there is pleasure and joy in looking at these flowers. This is the gratification in the case of the flowers, which are a type of material form.

Danger in the case of Material Form

So, what is the danger of material forms? The danger should also be understood. Buddha explains, *"Later, one might see that same girl as a woman at eighty, ninety or a hundred years of age; as crooked as a roof bracket, doubled up, supported by a walking stick, tottering, and frail; her youth has disappeared, her teeth broken, grey haired, scanty haired, bald, and wrinkled."* What has happened to her beauty? It has vanished!

So, Buddha asked, *"Has her former beauty and loveliness vanished and the danger become evident?"*

"Yes, Venerable Sir." replied the monks.

Try to see the danger in the case of material form. Buddha explains these concepts in detail. If someone has wisdom, and uses his wise consideration, then he will definitely be able to see and understand the danger. In another discourse in the Samyutta Nikāya 22:109, *the Sottāpanna Sutta,* Buddha explains that if someone has the knowledge of *the origin, the cessation, the gratification, the danger and the escape* of the Five Aggregates of Clinging, he is a Stream Entrant. This is why it is important for us to develop understanding and wisdom.

Then, let's consider that the same woman is now found afflicted, suffering, gravely ill, and lying on a bed in her own urine and excrement. What has happened to that beauty and loveliness? This is about our own life, isn't it? However, we generally don't try to understand this danger in our own life. We try to deny it and hide the truth. It's extremely important that we try to understand this as a Noble Truth.

We must understand our own bodies in this way: *'This material form is not mine. I am not this material form. This material form is not my self'.* This is the way we must understand. But if we think, *'This is mine. This I am. This is my self.',* then we will try to find gratification through the body.

Supreme Buddha then describes the same woman as a corpse, thrown aside onto a charnel ground, being eaten by crows, hawks, vultures, dogs, jackals and various kinds of worms. What has happened to that beauty? It has vanished. This is the danger in the case of material form. These are the things we have to understand, and this is *a very rare opportunity to gain wisdom.* In this world, the danger is not something that people try to understand, as people are always trying to find gratification and momentary satisfaction.

Buddha then describes the same woman as disconnected bones scattered in all directions, *"Here lies a hand bone. There lies a foot bone. Here lies a thigh bone. There lies a back bone. Here lies the skull."*

This is the knowledge and insight of the Supreme Buddha. If a person does not acquire this knowledge, even if that person has the opportunity to see for himself, he will not develop wisdom without that knowledge. He will only throw away the dead body and would not try to understand its true nature. If he thinks about the true nature of the dead body, then he is able to develop wisdom.

Lastly, Buddha describes the bones in a heap – bones that are more than a year old, decomposed and crumbled to dust. Buddha asks, *"What do you think, monks, has her former beauty and loveliness vanished and the dangers become evident?"*

This is the danger in the case of material forms. It's very important to keep these dangers in mind.

Escape in the case of Material Form

So what would be the escape in the case of material forms? It is *the removal of the desire and the lust towards material forms.* By fully understanding the dangers of material forms, we must abandon the desire and lust for material forms.

Gratification in the Case of Feeling

Buddha expained to the monks the gratification in the case of feeling by referring to the feelings experienced during meditation. If someone was to experience the meditative absorptions (the 1st, 2nd, 3rd, and 4th *jhānas*), secluded from sensual pleasure and from unwholesome states, there is a pleasant feeling. The feeling or pleasure derived through the *jhānas* in meditation is very important; and Buddha explains that, that kind of pleasure should be cultivated as the highest gratification in the case of feeling. So, if someone feels pleasure and joy through the feeling attained during meditative absorption, that pleasure and joy is the gratification in the case of feeling.

Danger in the Case of Feeling

What is the danger in the case of feeling? First let's consider the *cause* for feelings? The cause is *contact*. Are feelings permanent or impermanent? They are impermanent. With pleasant contact, pleasant feelings arise. With the cessation of pleasant contact, pleasant feelings will cease. This is the Doctrine. With the arising of unpleasant contact, unpleasant feelings will arise. With the cessation of unpleasant contact, the unpleasant feelings will cease. In the case of neutral feelings, with the arising of neutral contact, neutral feelings will arise. With the cessation of neutral contact, neutral feelings will cease. In this way, the Buddha explains that the danger in the case of feelings is that feelings are impermanent.

"Vedanā aniccam dukkam viparināmdammam. Ayam vedanāya ādīnavo." This means, *"feelings are impermanent, suffering, and subject to change: this is the danger in feelings."* You can understand any kind of feeling in the same way.

Escape in the Case of Feeling

Escape from feeling is *the removal of desire and lust towards feelings.* Can you remember at the beginning of this discourse, the other recluses asked about the difference between the Supreme Buddha's Dhamma and their own teachings? Buddha explained that if someone in this world doesn't understand things as they really are (gratification as gratification, danger as danger, escape as escape) in the case of sensual pleasures, material forms and feelings, it is impossible for them to instruct another.

The other recluses did not fully understand the nature of sensual pleasures, material forms and feelings, and therefore were not able to teach others, as Buddha was able to teach. Buddha further explains, if a recluse or teacher has the knowledge about things as they actually are (gratification as gratification, danger as danger, and escape as escape, in the case of sensual pleasures, in the case of material forms, and in the case of feelings), then it is possible for him to instruct another, as he has a *complete* understanding.

The Blessed One explained very clearly and the monks were satisfied and delighted with the Blessed One's words.

Question from a lay devotee:

"Did Supreme Buddha include the mind with the chords of sensual pleasure?"

Bhante:

In Buddha's discourses, Buddha explains only five chords as the chords of sensual pleasure. The mind-object is not to be taken as a sensual pleasure. When Buddha explains *the six internal faculties*, then Buddha includes the mind.

Panca Kamma Guna is the Five Chords of Sensual Pleasures. The *pleasure and joy* that arise in dependence of the five chords of sensual pleasure is gratification. Let's think about the Arahants. They live in this world, with beautiful forms, sounds, odours, tastes and tangibles. However, they have understood gratification, so there isn't craving (desire or lust) in their minds. The five chords of sensual pleasure are there, but gratification has been understood. Gratification means the pleasure and joy that arise because of the five chords of sensual pleasure.

Buddha was born with thirty-two marks which symbolize the characteristics of a great person. One of these great marks was the most sensitive experience of taste. The Buddha is one who experienced the richest and sweetest of flavours. Kings and other wealthy people offered very tasty and sweet alms-food to the Buddha. We also can prepare and eat very tasty and sweet foods. But when we eat, we must understand the gratification, and we must not crave or cling to the food as there is a danger in the very same food. This is the way a noble disciple must try to understand.

Relationship between the Five Hindrances and the Five Chords of Sensual Pleasure

The Five Hindrances are different from the Five Chords of Sensual Pleasure, but there is a connection between the two. They are related in that, craving for sensual pleasures will lead to hindrances. Also, if we have an aversion towards sensual pleasure, it will be a hindrance.

For example, if we are walking and see a friend of ours, what will arise? Remember, this friend is really a material form. In dependence of this material form, a desire or craving will arise towards that friend because we like that person. This is the first hindrance – sensual desire. If we see an enemy, what will arise? Hatred, ill will, aversion and other defilements will arise. The second of the Five Hindrances is ill will.

Comment from lay devotee:

"Although we want gratification to remain, we can not control it. Although we think that we are seeing a beautiful thing, we can not maintain that state, as it is subject to change."

Bhante:

Yes, that's what we need to understand. Everything is impermanent, subject to change, and brings suffering. If one can understand things in this way, he is a very wise person. He can face any incident, without crying and weeping, and without blaming others. If one tries to understand the nature of life in this way, there will be a useful framework in his life. He will enjoy sensual pleasures, but within a framework. Morality is the framework. Buddha does not say that a layperson must give up everything. He can enjoy through the five chords of sensual pleasure, but within the framework of morality. Monks are different, however. They have renounced the sensual world to investigate the Dhamma deeply and to develop along the Path faster than one could as a layperson.

Buddha used a simile to describe the life of an ordinary being and a noble disciple. The ordinary being swims with the flow of the river. But the noble disciple swims against the flow of the river. The river is a simile for sensual pleasures. Is it easy or difficult to swim against the flow of the river? It is very, very difficult. Ordinary people and friends will question as to why you are following precepts and meditating. They will advise you to enjoy life. When we watch television and read a newspaper, we will find lots of messages where people encourage us to enjoy sensual pleasures. However, now you have the knowledge and insight of the Supreme Buddha, our Great Teacher. You should be able to understand the gratification, danger and escape of sensual pleasures, material forms and feelings. Keep these teachings in mind as this Dhamma is the rare and perfect knowledge of our Supreme Buddha.

Sādhu! Sādhu! Sādhu!

May you have the opportunity to understand the Four Noble Truths in Gautama Sammā Sambuddha's Dispensation.

♋ Mālunkyaputta Sutta
Reject Sensuality

SAMYUTTA NIKĀYA 35:95

The discourse we are discussing today was addressed by the Supreme Buddha to a Bhikkhu named Mālunkyaputta, hence it is called the Mālunkyaputta Sutta.

If You Are Seeking Liberation

You may have heard of a discourse addressed by the Tathāgatha to a hermit named Bāhiya Dārucīriya (Bāhiya of the Bark-cloth) Ud 1:10. Bāhiya lived in a hermitage, in a region called Suppāraka, which is close to modern day Bombay. Bāhiya had a habit of wearing clothes made of splinters of wood. As he was a hermit and wore this unusual outfit, the people of the area thought he was an odd, but special being. They began to respect him, treat him well, and even pay homage to him. Bāhiya became proud of his achievements. He thought if there are *Arahants (Liberated Ones)* in this world, he too was one of them.

One day, a deity who had once been a blood relative of Bāhiya, realized Bāhiya's mistaken belief and appeared before him. The deity said, *"Bāhiya, though you think you have attained Arahantship (Liberation), you have not, nor do you know the way to attain Arahantship."* Bāhiya realized the truth of what the deity said and replied, *"Sir, please let me know where the Arahants dwell, and those who know the way to attain liberation".* The deity replied, *"In Sāvatthi, at the monastery in Jeta's Grove, dwells The Exalted One who has attained Arahantship without the help of a teacher. He is the Sammā Sambuddha, the rightly Self-Awakened One. He will teach you the way to attain liberation".* On hearing this, Bāhiya was extremely happy and was impatient to meet the Supreme Buddha.

There are six qualities that should be developed by anyone who is wishing to understand the Dhamma (*AN 6:88 Sussūsa Sutta*):

- *sussūsati* – he desires to listen to the Dhamma,
- *sotam odahati* – he listens to the Dhamma with close attention,
- *aññāya cittam upatthāpeti* – he applies the mind with determination to realize the Dhamma,
- *attham ganhāti* – he has the ability to grasp what is expounded in the Dhamma,
- *anattham riñcati* – he can eliminate what is inapplicable, and
- *anulomikāya khantiyā samannāgato hoti* – he has the ability to understand the Dhamma by applying it to oneself.

Fortunately Bāhiya had all these qualities.

The Buddha I Am Searching For

Early the next morning, Bāhiya left for Sāvatthi. Sāvatthi was thousands of miles away. Bāhiya, impatient to meet the Buddha, did not waste time. He spent only a single night in each of the villages he traveled through. Finally, he reached the city of Sāvatthi. He went directly to Jeta's Grove, Anāthapindika's

Monastery. A bhikkhu informed him that the Buddha had gone begging for alms. Then Bāhiya hurriedly went to the city of Sāvatthi. He searched for the Blessed One in the city. There were many bhikkhus collecting alms. In the midst, he saw the Blessed One going for alms – calmly, senses restrained, accomplished and trained. He recognized and said to himself, *"There He is, there He is, the Buddha I am searching for".* He approached the Blessed One and on reaching him, threw himself down to the ground and said, *"Teach me the Dhamma, Venerable Sir. Teach me the Dhamma".*

In Brief for the Wise

The Buddha had the exceptional quality of being able to direct his discourse in the most appropriate manner – like an arrow that meets its target. The Blessed One said to Bāhiya, *"Then, Bāhiya, you should train yourself in this way: in reference to the seen, there will be only 'the seen'; in reference to the heard, only 'the heard'; in reference to the sensed, only 'the sensed'; in reference to the cognized, only 'the cognized'. That is how you should train yourself. Then, Bāhiya, there is no 'you' in terms of that. Where there is no 'you' in terms of that, there is no 'you' there. When there is no 'you' there, 'you' are neither here, nor beyond, nor between the two. This is the end of suffering".* After having exhorted Bāhiya with this brief explanation of the Dhamma, the Blessed One left for alms.

Bāhiya sat down and contemplated with perfect wisdom as to what the Buddha expounded. In a short while, he was able to understand the truth. He discerned the Four Noble Truths and achieved Arahantship. Not long after the Blessed One's departure, Bāhiya was attacked by a cow and lost his life. On returning from the alms round with the monks, the Blessed One saw the dead body of Bāhiya on the wayside. The Tathāgata instructed the monks to take Bāhiya's body, cremate it, and build a memorial. Thereafter the Blessed One said, *"Monks, Bāhiya was wise and extremely clever. He realized the Dhamma. He has attained Nibbāna. He is totally unbound."*

In Brief for the Young

The other fortunate bhikkhu who heard this wonderful discourse on another occasion was Bhikkhu Mālunkyaputta. Mālunkyaputta was an aged bhikkhu. Eventhough he was physically old, his mind was very alert. He was a wise bhikkhu. He said to the Blessed One, *"Venerable Sir, I like to dwell alone, in seclusion renouncing all attachments, and lead a holy life. Please advise the way to realize the Dhamma. I like to listen to a brief discourse"*. Then the Tathāgata replied, *"Mālunkyaputta, if a person of your age asks for instructions in brief, what should I say to the young?"* The Buddha said this to encourage Mālunkyaputta. Mālunkyaputta accepted the challenge and said, *"Venerable Sir, eventhough I am old, I could understand the Dhamma. Please deliver a brief discourse"*. Then the Blessed One asked Mālunkyaputta the following questions.

Because You Have Seen

"What do you think, Mālunkyaputta, do you have any desire, lust or fondness for objects cognizable by the eye that you have not seen before, that you do not see now, and would not think will be seen?" Mālunkyaputta replied, *"No indeed, Venerable Sir, I do not have any desire, lust or fondness for them"*.

The same questions were asked regarding sounds, smells, flavours, tangibles and mental objects. The answers were similar. Now we should be able to understand to some extent that attachment and desire for visible objects, sounds, scents, flavors, tangibles and mental objects arise due to past experiences. Was it not after we learned of *Nibbāna* that we realized the need to attain *Nibbāna*?

What is *samsāra*? Is it far, is it near or is it available here? It is only a name given to the continuation of life from one existence to another due to attachment and desire for visible objects, sounds, smells, tastes, tangibles, and mental objects. The Blessed One expounded to Mālunkyaputta the same discourse preached to Bāhiya.

There Will Only Be the Seen

"Mālunkyaputta, be mindful of what I say: in reference to the seen, there will be only 'the seen' (ditthe ditthamattam bhavissati); in reference to the heard, only 'the heard' (sute sutamattam bhavissati); in reference to the sensed, only 'the sensed' (mute mutamattam bhavissati); in reference to the cognized, only 'the cognized' (viññāte viññātamattam bhavissati)."

"Then, Mālunkyaputta, if you realize this, you will be freed of dependent-arising. If there is no dependent-arising, there is no 'you' in terms of that. When there is no 'you' in terms of that, there is no 'you' there. When there is no 'you' there, you are neither here, nor beyond, nor between the two. Then, you would be liberated".

Bhikkhu Mālunkyaputta understood fully the meaning of what the Buddha stated in brief. Eventhough he was an aged bhikkhu, he realized with wisdom the truth of what the Buddha said. This discourse could be understood by reading Dhamma stanzas. They show us the cause of suffering, the cessation of suffering and the way to attain *Nibbāna*.

Nibbāna is Far Away

The following stanzas (originally in Pali; and that have been translated into English) explain the cause of suffering and the continuation of life from one existence to another:

- "Forms seen, will cause the loss of mindfulness if one dwells on their endearing charms. Then, the passion that grips the heart is enjoyed with a clinging desire. Diverse feelings grow, centered on the form that was perceived. Then, the mind is defiled by desire and dissatisfaction. This leads to suffering. Thus for him, *Nibbāna* is far away."

- "Sounds heard, will cause the loss of mindfulness if one dwells on their endearing charms. Then, the passion that grips the heart is enjoyed with a clinging desire. Diverse feelings grow, centered on the sound that was heard. Then, the mind is defiled by desire and dissatisfaction. This leads to suffering. Thus for him, *Nibbāna* is far away."

- "Aromas smelled, will cause the loss of mindfulness if one dwells on their endearing charms. Then, the passion that grips the heart is enjoyed with a clinging desire. Diverse feelings grow, centered on the aromas smelled. Then, the mind is defiled by desire and dissatisfaction. This leads to suffering. Thus for him, *Nibbāna* is far away."

- "Flavours tasted, will cause the loss of mindfulness if one dwells on their endearing charms. Then, the passion that grips the heart is enjoyed with a clinging desire. Diverse feelings grow, centered on the flavours tasted. Then, the mind is defiled by desire and dissatisfaction. This leads to suffering. Thus for him, *Nibbāna* is far away."

- "Tangibles touched, will cause the loss of mindfulness if one dwells on their endearing charms. Then, the passion that grips the heart is enjoyed with a clinging desire. Diverse feelings grow, centered on the tangibles touched. Then, the mind is defiled by desire and dissatisfaction. This leads to suffering. Thus for him, *Nibbāna* is far away."

- "Mental objects cognized, will cause the loss of mindfulness if one dwells on their endearing charms. Then, the passion that grips the heart is enjoyed with a clinging desire. Diverse feelings grow, centered on the mental objects cognized. Then, the mind is defiled by desire and dissatisfaction. This leads to suffering. Thus for him, *Nibbāna* is far away."

It is Better to Be a Beggar

There are some women who think it is fortunate to be born a male. They have a mistaken belief that as a male, they could acquire more merit. There was a beautiful woman name Isidāsī. She was a very virtuous woman and was from a rich family. After marrying, she cared for her husband, but he did not return that love to her. He quarreled with her, and one day he chased her out of the house taking half of her wealth. Isidāsī went back to her parents' home. Her parents gave her in marriage for the second time, but her marriage failed again. Isidāsī was very miserable. One day her father saw a young man begging in the street. He called him and said, *"Give up begging and live in my house. I have a daughter whom you could marry, and you can look after my property"*. The young man was very happy with the suggestion. Isidāsī thought she could now live in peace. Unfortunately, this marriage was also a failure. Her husband said, *"It is better to be a beggar."*, and he deserted her. Isidāsī was very miserable and she was disgusted with life. One day, an

Arahant (a Liberated One) named Bhikkhuni Nagadatta, visited Isidāsī. Isidāsī got permission from her parents to become a bhikkhuni. Isidāsī realized that she had now chosen the correct path. Very soon, she understood the Dhamma and attained Arahantship (Thi. 400-47).

Arahant Bikkhuni Isidāsī thought about her life. She became aware of the cause of her suffering. She realized seven births prior to her current birth, she had been born a male. During that life he had molested young girls. After his death, he was born in hell. He suffered in hell for a considerable period of time. Next, he was born as a monkey. He was attacked by an older monkey and was wounded. The wound festered and did not heal for a long time. Finally, the monkey died after much suffering. His unfortunate *kamma* was not over. He was born as a goat and next, as a cow, and suffered similar fates in those lives as well. Thereafter, he was born a human being; a female. Her mother was a low-caste poor servant. One day, debtors took the young girl away from the mother, and her life ended thus. Finally, she was fortunate to be born during the time of the Buddha, and was liberated from the sufferings of *samsāra*. Therefore, we all should realize that we need to reform ourselves by conforming to the Dhamma, if we are to attain liberation.

Nibbāna Is Very Near

Let's now continue with the short discourse expounded by the Buddha to Mālunkyaputta. Mālunkyaputta understood in full the meaning of what the Blessed One had stated in brief. He realized in the following manner that the four foundations of mindfulness *(satipatthāna)* should be developed and pursued if one is to be liberated.

- "He who dwells mindfully does not get aroused by the things he sees. Seeing forms, he retains his mindfulness and simply feels with non-attachment. In him, there is no clinging. He just observes the forms he sees without any reaction towards them. Demolishing the pile (of defilements), without building up, he proceeds mindfully. As he is not storing pain and affliction, *Nibbāna* is very near for him."

- "He who dwells mindfully does not get aroused by the sounds he hears. Hearing sounds he retains his mindfulness and simply feels with non-attachment. In him, there is no clinging. He just listens to the sounds he hears without any reaction towards them. Demolishing the pile, without building up, he proceeds mindfully. As he is not storing pain and affliction, *Nibbāna* is very near for him."

- "He who dwells mindfully does not get aroused by the aromas he smells. Smelling aromas he retains his mindfulness and simply feels with non-attachment. In him, there is no clinging. He just smells the aromas without any reaction towards them. Demolishing the pile, without building up, he proceeds mindfully. As he is not storing pain and affliction, *Nibbāna* is very near for him."

- "He who dwells mindfully does not get aroused by the flavours he tastes. Tasting flavours, he retains his mindfulness and simply feels with non-attachment. In him, there is no clinging. He just tastes the flavours without any reaction towards them. Demolishing the pile, without building up, he proceeds mindfully. As he is not storing pain and affliction, *Nibbāna* is very near for him."

- "He who dwells mindfully does not get aroused by the tangibles he touches. Touching tangibles, he retains his mindfulness and simply feels with non-attachment. In him, there is no clinging. He just touches the tangibles without any reaction towards them. Demolishing the pile, without building up, he proceeds mindfully. As he is not storing pain and affliction, *Nibbāna* is very near for him."

- "He who dwells mindfully does not get aroused by the mental objects he cognizes. Cognizing mental objects, he retains his mindfulness and simply feels with non-attachment. In him, there is no clinging. He just cognizes the mental objects without any reaction towards them. Demolishing the pile, without building up, he proceeds mindfully. As he is not storing pain and affliction, *Nibbāna* is very near for him."

We should now be able to understand the deep meaning of the phrase: *in the seen, there will only be 'the seen'.* Similarly, *in the heard, only 'the heard'; in the sensed, only 'the sensed'; in the cognized, only 'the cognized'.* Do not welcome them, and do not persist in clinging to them.

Mālunkyaputta said, *"Venerable Sir, I understand fully, the meaning of what the Blessed One has stated in brief."* The Blessed One then said, *"Sādhu, sādhu, Malukyaputta, you have understood the Dhamma. You have realized the Dhamma".*

Thereafter, Mālunkyaputta lived a secluded life renouncing worldly pleasures; ardent and resolute in attaining *Nibbāna*. Detached from craving, he remained focused on the four foundations of mindfulness. Soon, he became an *Arahant*.

Liberation through One's *Sīla, Samādhi, Paññā*

This discourse teaches us the way to dwell in the four foundations of mindfulness in order to eradicate suffering. We should be aware that visible objects, sounds, scents, tastes, tangibles and thoughts are *impermanent, unsatisfactory and without self.* Realizing that all conditioned things are impermanent, unsatisfactory and without self, is achieved through insight meditation.

The Buddha-Dhamma yields results. It is not merely of theoretical significance. If we regret or indulge in mental worries, we will not be liberated from suffering.

The Blessed One explained using a simile, that very few persons would understand the Dhamma. The Buddha placed a minute amount of sand from the earth on the top of a fingernail and said, *"As minute as this quantity of sand is, in comparison to that of the entire earth, this would be the quantity of people, in comparison to that of the entire world, that will realize the Dhamma."* If during the time of the Buddha so few understood and realized the true and pure Dhamma, then in the present day, with many various inaccurate interpretations of the Dhamma, we need to be extremely careful not to be misled by those misinterpretations of the Dhamma.

We should realize that according to the Doctrine, *dependent on the arranging of kamma, birth arises (bhava paccayā jāti).* That is, the *kamma*-process, or actions, and the *kamma*-resultant rebirth process, is the condition for birth. In this way, life continues from one existence to another.

Therefore, with morality *(sīla)*, concentration *(samādhi)*, and wisdom *(paññā)*, one should dwell in the four foundations of mindfulness to eradicate the mass of suffering and attain Liberation.

Sādhu! Sādhu! Sādhu!

May you have the opportunity to understand the Four Noble Truths in Gautama Sammā Sambuddha's Dispensation.

∽ *Gautama Sutta*
The Blessed One's Investigative Struggle for Enlightenment

SAMYUTTA NIKĀYA 12:10

Venerable Maha Sangha and meritorious disciples, today we are going to discuss a discourse from the Samyutta Nikāya. The name of this discourse is Gautama Sutta.

Supreme Buddha has taught us the importance of *saddhā*. *Saddhā* means having a pleasant mind towards, and confidence, in the Supreme Buddha. This confidence should be rooted (*mūlajāta*), and it should be well established (*patitthita*). To develop this kind of unshakeable confidence, it is important to know about the knowledge of the Supreme Buddha. By learning the Dhamma, the Supreme Buddha's Teachings, we can learn about the knowledge of the Supreme Buddha.

The Noble Dhamma has a special quality. In Pāli, it is *'paññāvantassa ayam dhammo; nāyam dhammo duppaññassa'* which means, *'this Dhamma is for the wise; not for the unwise'* (*AN* 8:30). If the listener is wise, then he will be able to cultivate a pleasant mind by hearing and learning the Dhamma. Therefore, when we talk about *saddhā*, confidence or pleasant mind, we are speaking about confidence in the *knowledge of the Supreme Buddha*.

Our goal as a noble disciple is to understand the Four Noble Truths in the dispensation of Gautama Supreme Buddha. To understand the Four Noble Truths, the initial factor is associating with noble friends. With the association of noble friends, one will be able to listen to the true Dhamma. Then, a noble disciple develops wise consideration to understand the Four Noble Truths. Gradually, one will be able to achieve the goal: The Noble Truth of suffering will be understood; the origin of suffering, as a Noble Truth, will be eradicated; the cessation of suffering, as a Noble Truth, will be achieved; and, the Path leading to the cessation of suffering, as a Noble Truth, will be followed. This is the goal of a noble disciple.

From today's discourse, we can learn about the Gautama Supreme Buddha's struggle to attain Enlightenment, and about the research of our Great Teacher, while still a Bodhisatta. By understanding the key landmarks of that research and the various kinds of knowledge attained, our confidence in the Supreme Buddha can be further developed.

Even before attaining Enlightenment, Prince Siddhartha, in his prime youth, had great insight. He considered thus: *'In this world, all beings, being themselves subject to birth, aging, illness, sorrow and death, are seeking the same thing. They are seeking what is subject to birth, what is subject to aging, what is subject to illness, what is subject to sorrow, and what is subject to death.'*

Then, he considered his own life: *'What am I doing? Being subject to aging, illness, death, sorrow, and defilements, what is it that I am seeking?'*

These thoughts and questions occurred to him while still living in the palace as a Prince: *'What is the purpose of this life and its struggles? At the end of life, there will be death.'*

After Enlightenment, Buddha understood that this is a particular type of research. He, himself, subject to aging and death, seeks that, which is also subject to aging and death. This is a research and it is called **ignoble research** *(anariya pariyesanā)*. This kind of research is predominant in the world.

Even while living a luxurious life in the palace, he thought, *'I want to escape from this ordinary situation. I want to find the unborn, the un-aging, the deathless, sorrowless – real happiness.'* He understood this is also a type of research. It is called **noble research** *(ariya pariyesanā)*. We are fortunate today, as we can learn about that noble research, proclaimed by our Great Teacher. Otherwise, we would continue with our ignoble research, being born again and again, in this endless *samsāra*.

When the Bodhisatta abandoned all luxuries and renounced to find an answer to his question, there was no one there to teach him. The Bodhisatta struggled for six years, searching for teachers and pursuing ascetic practices. From this experience, he understood there are two extremes in this world: the extreme of sensual pleasures and the extreme of self-mortification. At that time, there wasn't a teacher to teach him about these extremes, so he had to experience and learn about them himself.

At the end of that six year time period, one day, he sat under a tree. This tree was called the Bodhi Tree. He thought, *'Until I attain Enlightenment, I do not want to stand up from this spot.'* He did not know what to do to attain Enlightenment, but he had meditation as a tool *(ānāpānasati* – breathing meditation). Then, with incomparable effort, incomparable mindfulness, and incomparable wisdom, he gradually developed his concentration.

With concentration, a special knowledge arose in his mind. He had developed the knowledge about his past lives. This knowledge is called *the recollection of past lives (pubbenivāsānussati ñāna)*. From that knowledge, he clearly understood that there is a long journey called *samsāra*, and it is the cycle of birth and death. He had the realization: *'I have been born in the animal world, in the ghost world, in the human world, and in the heavenly world so many times, and the beginning point cannot be seen. There is an undiscoverable beginning point.'* This was the first knowledge that arose in the Bodhisatta.

A special faculty was developed: *the divine eye.* He could see things that could not be seen by the ordinary physical eye. From the first knowledge, he saw the journey of his own lives. Then he thought, *'What is the situation of other beings?'* He developed his concentration further and a second knowledge arose in him. He saw that all beings are on the same journey, the endless cycle of birth and death. This knowledge is called *the knowledge of the passing away and reappearing of beings (cutūpapātha ñāna).* In seeing this, there was great compassion and sympathy in his mind. As a Bodhisatta, he had attained two kinds of knowledge: the recollection of past lives and the passing away and reappearing of beings. This discourse begins at that point in time.

Before attaining Enlightenment, still as a Bodhisatta, he considered thus: *'Sadly, this world and all beings are in great danger. All beings are born, age, pass away and are reborn again and again, but no one knows how to escape from this mass of suffering. When will these beings escape from suffering, aging and death?'*

Beings travel from one world to another world; are reborn, are aging, and passing away. But, how many are thinking about the reason why this is happening? The Bodhisatta thought about the reason for aging and death, and what conditions aging and death. Pay careful attention to this, as this is the way our Great Teacher understood the Four Noble Truths, and this is the same way a noble disciple follows, to escape from *samsāra*.

First, the Bodhisatta achieved purification of body, speech and mind. This is called virtue or morality *(sīla)*. Because of this blameless life, he was able to develop his mind. Morality helps to develop concentration *(samādhi)*. Having developed his concentration to the fourth jhāna, he then developed the third factor – wisdom *(paññā)*. We now know that these are the three factors of the Noble Eightfold Path (virtue, concentration and wisdom), but at that time, a Noble Eightfold Path was not known.

Having achieved virtue and concentration, the Bodhisatta was trying to develop wisdom. As a result of wise consideration, he developed wisdom and understood that because of birth, aging and death arise. *Jāti paccayā jarāmaranam* – **dependent on birth, aging and death arise.** This is a marvelous discovery. Without the knowledge of the Supreme Buddha, no one would know the reason for this suffering. What is the reason for this mental suffering, physical suffering, aging and death? *Birth* is the reason. But most human beings in the world, are wishing for another birth, due to ignorant minds *(avijjā)*.

Later, he understood the meaning of birth. Birth means obtaining an eye, an ear, a nose, a tongue, a body and a mind. Obtaining six faculties, is birth. If there are these six faculties, there will be aging and death. Then, the Bodhisatta considered the next question: what is the reason for birth; what conditions birth? Because of his wise consideration and wisdom, he understood that when there is an arranging of *kamma (bhava)*, there is birth. He understood that no one creates birth; and birth is not by chance. This birth is not according to one's own wish. There is a reason for this birth, and the reason is *bhava*, the arranging of *kamma*. When a being performs actions with body, speech and mind, then there is the arranging of *kamma* for another birth.

Bhava paccayā jati – dependent on the arranging of kamma, birth arises. The arranging of *kamma* is the reason for birth.

As we continue to look further at Dependent Arising, you will be able to clearly understand how the arising of an eye, and all the other faculties, is due to old *kamma*. If a being has acted in a wholesome manner, there will be birth in a pleasant world: in the heaven or human world. If they have acted in an unwholesome manner, by body, speech and mind, then there will be a birth in an unpleasant world: in hell, the ghost world or animal world.

The next question considered by the Bodhisatta, was finding the reason for the arranging of *kamma*. He understood that *clinging* is the reason for the arranging of kamma. *Upādāna paccayā bhavo – dependent on clinging, the arranging of kamma arises.* Clinging is the reason for the arranging of *kamma*. Clinging conditions the arranging of *kamma*.

However, the Bodhisatta didn't stop there. He understood that there are four kinds of clinging:

- *Kāmūpādāna* is the clinging to sensual pleasures: clinging to beautiful forms, smells, tastes, sounds, and tangibles. Because of clinging to these sensual pleasures, there is the arranging of *kamma*.

- *Ditthūpādāna* is the clinging to views: clinging to one's own wrong views, and thinking those views are the only truth. Because of clinging to views, there arises the arranging of *kamma*.

- *Sīlabbatūpādāna* is the clinging to rituals and observances, and

* *Attavādupādāna* is the clinging to a self-view, as a result of not knowing the cause and effect process; the view that there is an eternal person or *self* in this life, and that it can be controlled.

So, these four kinds of clinging condition the arranging of *kamma*.

The Bodhisatta continued with his research, by asking, *'What is the reason for this clinging; what conditions clinging?'* He understood that when there is craving, there is clinging. *Tanhā paccayā upādāna – dependent on craving, clinging arises.* The Supreme Buddha realized that beings cling to sensual pleasures because they have a craving for sensual pleasures. They want to enjoy with sensual pleasures. The craving for forms, sounds, smells, tastes, tangibles, (and mind-objects), conditions clinging.

Again, the Bodhisatta did not stop the noble research. He wanted to understand all the roots of this suffering. *'What is the reason for this craving? What conditions craving?'* Because of his wise consideration and wisdom, he understood that *feeling* is the reason for craving. When beings see forms, smell odours, taste flavours, hear sounds, touch tangibles, and think thoughts, there is a gratification or pleasant feeling; and desire arises. They do whatever is necessary to fulfill that gratification – engage in good actions or bad actions, good speech or bad speech, good thoughts or bad thoughts. This is the arranging of *kamma* that brings about another birth.

Vedanā paccayā tanhā – dependent on feeling, craving arises. Where are the feelings? They are based in the six faculties. When one sees a form with the eye, or hears a sound with the ear, there will be a feeling based on that contact. There are six different bases of feeling: feeling born from the contact of eye, feeling born from the contact of ear, feeling born from the contact of nose, feeling born from the contact of tongue, feeling born from the contact of body, and feeling born from the contact of mind.

The Bodhisatta then considered the reason for these feelings. Because of the Teachings of the Supreme Buddha, we now know the answers to all these questions. But, under that Bodhi Tree, the Supreme Buddha, alone, struggled to discover these answers. The Supreme Buddha did not abandon the struggle, even in the face of Māra (the Evil One) and his troops.

Supreme Buddha next understood *phassa paccayā vedanā – dependent on contact, feeling arises.* The reason for feeling is contact. There are six kinds of contact. Contact of eye is the coming together and meeting of: eye, form and consciousness of eye. When we close our eyes, there is no contact of the eye, as consciousness of eye is not there at that moment to cognize a form. When there is the meeting of the three factors for contact of eye, then feeling arises. The same is true for contact with the other five faculties: ear, nose, tongue, body and mind.

As a Bodhisattha, he then thought, *'Why is there the meeting of three factors, and why can't I escape contact?'* *Salāyatana paccayā phasso – dependent on the six faculties, contact arises.* The six faculties are the reason for contact. If there was not an eye, there wouldn't be the meeting of eye, form and consciousness of eye for contact of eye to arise.

Again, he considered, *'What is the reason for these six faculties'*? The Bodhisattha discovered that mentality-materiality *(nāma-rūpa)* is the reason for the six faculties. **Mentality *(nāma)*** is made up of: feeling, perception, volition, contact and attention *(vedanā, saññā, cetanā, passa, manasikāra)*. **Materiality *(rūpa)*,** the physical form, is made up of the four great elements. He understood that eye, for example, is made up of the earth element, the water element, the heat element and the air element. In a dead body, there are these four great elements, but it is not sufficient to travel through this *saṃsāra*. The six faculties need to be alive. There needs to be mentality *(nāma)*. *Nāma rūpa paccayā salāyatanam* – **dependent on mentality-materiality, six faculties arise.** Mentality-materiality conditions the six faculties.

The Bodhisatta then considered, *'What is the reason for mentality-materiality?'* We are not able to simply examine the eye itself, or any of the faculties, to discover the reality and truth that were discovered by the Supreme Buddha. *Wisdom* needs to be developed to see the true nature of the six faculties. Because of his wisdom, the Bodhisatta understood that when there is consciousness, there is mentality-materiality.

There are six kinds of consciousness: consiousness of eye, consciousness of ear, consciousness of nose, consciousness of tongue, consciousness of body, and consciousness of mind. Because of consciousness, mentality and materiality arise. For example, in order to cognize a form, there should be attention to the form. When attention is there, consciousness arises. When there is consciousness, there is contact (the meeting of eye, form and consciousness of eye).

When contact is there, these three things are born: feeling, perception and volition *(vedanā, saññā, and cetanā)*. These three things are born dependent on contact. Therefore, when there is consciousness, all these factors arise: attention, contact, volition, perception and feeling, with a combination of the four great elements. Mentality *(nāma)* consists of: feeling, perception, volition, contact, and attention – the same factors. *Viññāṇam paccayā nāma-rūpam* – **dependent on consciousness, mentality and materiality arise.**

The Bodhisatta then wanted to know the reason for consciousness? The reason for consciousness is the three kinds of *sankhāra*: bodily *(kāya) sankhāra,* verbal *(vacī) sankhāra,* mental *(citta) sankhāra.*

- **kāya sankhāra** is *'in and out breathing',* bound to body,
- **vacī sankhāra** is *'applied and sustained thought',* expressed in words, bound in speech, and
- **citta sankhāra** is *'perception and feeling',* bound with mind (Cula Vedalla Sutta – MN43).

Because of these processes, consciousness arises. *Sankhāra paccayā viññanam* – **dependent on sankhāra, consciousness arises.** *Sankhāra* conditions consciousness.

The Bodhisatta then asked, *'What is the reason for these three types of sankhāra?'* *Avijjā paccayā sankhāra* – **dependent on ignorance, sankhāra arises.** Ignorance is the reason for this ignorant body; ignorance is the reason for this ignorant speech; and ignorance is the reason for this ignorant mind. Ignorance is: not knowing suffering, not knowing the origin of suffering, not knowing the cessation of suffering, and not knowing the path leading to the cessation of suffering, as Noble Truths.

We have that ignorance. Have we understood this body or is this an ignorant body? This is an ignorant body. And, why do we tell lies? It is because there is ignorance in our speech. Why is there mental suffering? It is because there is ignorance in our mind. There is distorted perception and feeling – without understanding.

So, let's carefully consider all of this for a moment. There is *sankhāra (kāya sankhāra, vacī sankhāra and citta sankhāra),* and when we open our eyes, consciousness arises with ignorance. With the six faculties, six kinds of consciousness arise.

Avijjā paccayā saṅkhāra – dependent on ignorance, *saṅkhāra* arises. And, *saṅkhāra paccayā viññāṇam* – *dependent on saṅkhāra, consciousness arises.* *Viññāṇa paccayā nāma-rūpam* – dependent on consciousness, mentality and materiality arise. With such ignorant mentality-materiality, we have six faculties. *Nāma rūpa paccayā salāyatanam* – dependent on mentality-materiality, six faculties arise. *Salāyatana paccayā phasso* – dependent on the six faculties, contact arises.

Therefore, when we open our eyes, we are seeing forms with ignorance. We hear sounds with ignorance. We smell odours with ignorance. We taste with ignorance. We experience tangibles with ignorance, and we think thoughts with ignorance. And with ignorant contact, feeling arises (*passa paccayā vedanā* – dependent on contact, feeling arises).

Furthermore, when feeling arises, dependent on that feeling, craving arises (*vedanā paccayā tanhā* – dependent on feeling, craving arises). We have craving or desire because of the gratification of that feeling. We have the desire to experience the gratification of beautiful forms, sounds, etc... with the internal faculties. Then, dependent on that craving, we cling (*tanhā paccayā upādānam* – dependent on craving, clinging arises).

We then use our body, speech and mind to enjoy those things. This is called the arranging of *kamma* (*upādāna paccayā bhavo* – dependent on clinging, the arranging of *kamma* arises). And finally, because of the arranging of *kamma*, birth arises (*bhava paccayā jāti* – dependent on the arranging of *kamma*, birth arises).

When we die here, we will be born somewhere, whether we like to or not. And, the birth is not according to our choice. It is according to *kamma*. Then, as we know, when there is birth, there is aging and death (*jāti paccayā jarāmaraṇam* – dependent on birth, aging and death arise). In this way, there is the arising of the whole mass of suffering.

This understanding is called *'the light'* about the origin of suffering. The Bodhisatta concluded and thought: *"Samudayo, samudayo ti kho bhikkave."* – *"This is the origin, this is the origin."* *"Pube ananussutesu dhammesu."* – *"This knowledge has never been attained before".*

With that knowledge, the eye of Dhamma arose in him *(cakkum udapādi)*; knowledge arose *(ñānam udapādi)*; wisdom arose *(paññā udapādi)*; true knowledge arose *(vijjā udapādi)*; and light arose *(āloko udapādi)*.

Can you appreciate why our Great Teacher is called *Sammā Sambuddha*? The Supreme Buddha understood the origin of suffering, without anyone's help. Was there a teacher to teach the Supreme Buddha? No. There wasn't a teacher. The Supreme Buddha, alone, discovered the origin of suffering.

However, the Bodhisatta did not finish his research there. What was the Bodhisatta's next question? *"With the cessation of what, does aging and death cease?"* The Bodhisatta understood that when there is not birth, there is not aging and death. **With the cessation of birth, there is the cessation of aging and death** *(jāti nirodhā, jarā marana nirodho)*.

Therefore, as long as there is birth with eyes, ears, nose, tongue, body and mind, we will not be released from suffering. With these ignorant six faculties, no one can escape from suffering. However, if we can understand these six faculties, then in this life itself, here and now, we can escape from suffering, and there will not be another birth with another six faculties. This is the cessation of suffering.

Then the Bodhisatta considered: *'With the cessation of what, does birth cease?'* The Bodhisatta understood from wise consideration and his developed wisdom, that if there is not the arranging of *kamma*, there will not be birth *(bhava nirodha, jāti nirodho)*. **With the cessation of the arranging of kamma, birth ceases.**

The Bodhisatta then wanted to know: *'With the cessation of what, does the arranging of kamma cease?'* What is the reason for the arranging of *kamma*? We now know that it is *clinging*. He understood that when there is not clinging, there is not the arranging of *kamma*. **With the cessation of clinging, the arranging of kamma ceases** *(upādāna nirodhā bhava nirodho)*.

He then considered the question: *'With the cessation of what, does clinging cease?'* When there is not craving, there is not clinging. **With the cessation of craving, clinging ceases** *(tanhā nirodhā upādāna nirodho)*.

"With the cessation of what, does craving cease?" When there is not feeling, there is not craving. **With the cessation of feeling, craving ceases** *(vedanā nirodhā tanhā nirodho)*.

Then, he considered, *'With the cessation of what, does feeling cease?"* If there is not contact, there is not feeling. **With the cessation of contact, feeling ceases** *(phassa nirodhā vedanā nirodho)*. Can we have a feeling without contact? We now understand that we cannot have a feeling without contact.

Can we escape from feeling if there is contact? No, we cannot. So, with the cessation of what, does contact cease? **With the cessation of the six faculties, contact ceases** *(salāyatana nirodhā phassa nirodho)*. When there are not the ignorant six faculties, there is no ignorant contact.

With wise consideration and developed wisdom, he then questioned: *'With the cessation of what, do these six faculties then cease?'* When there is not mentality-materiality, there are not the six faculties. **With the cessation of mentality-materiality, there is the cessation of six faculties** *(nāma-rūpa nirodhā salāyatana nirodho).*

'With the cessation of what, comes the cessation of mentality and materiality?' If there is not consciousness, there is not mentality-materiality. **With the cessation of consciousness, mentality-materiality ceases** *(viññāna nirodhā nāma-rūpa nirodho).*

Then, *'with the cessation of what, does consciousness cease?'* **With the cessation of the three kinds of sankhāra, there comes the cessation of consciousness** *(sankhāra nirodhā viññāna nirodho).*

'With the cessation of what, does sankhāra cease?' The Bodhisatta understood that when there is not ignorance, there is not *sankhāra* (that is, *ignorant sankhāra*). **With the cessation of ignorance, sankhāra ceases** *(avijjā nirodhā sankhāra nirodho).*

The Bodhisatta then understood that if there is the cessation of ignorance, it is the greatest thing. The opposite of ignorance is true knowledge. In Pāli it is called *vijjā*. The meaning of true knowledge is *knowledge and understanding of the Four Noble Truths.*

First, the Bodhisatta had the knowledge of suffering as a Noble Truth. Then, he understood the origin of suffering as a Noble Truth. Next, he understood the cessation of suffering as a Noble Truth. He attained all this while still sitting under that same Bodhi Tree. At this point, he has completed the path of virtue, concentration and wisdom. He has followed The Noble Eightfold Path. There wasn't any teacher to help him. Alone, he has achieved true knowledge. Though there is a body, there is not ignorance. It is a fully understood body. This is the life of an

Arahant. Though he speaks words, he does not speak false speech. He has knowledge about speech. His mind is a fully purified mind. All ignorant *sankhāras* have ceased.

Sankhāra nirodhā, viññāna nirodho – with the cessation of *sankhāra*, consciousness ceases. *Viññāna nirodhā, nāma-rūpa nirodho* – with the cessation of consciousness, mentality-materiality ceases. *Nāma rūpa nirodhā, salāyatana nirodho* – with the cessation of mentality-materiality, the six faculties cease. In the case of the Supreme Buddha, after Enlightenment, as an Arahant, there was consciousness, mentality-materiality and the six faculties, but there was not *ignorance*. He lived on this Earth, and there was contact, but it was not *ignorant contact*.

Salāyatana nirodhā phassa nirodho – with the cessation of six faculties, contact ceases. *Passa nirodha vedanā nirodho* – with the cessation of contact, feeling ceases. The Supreme Buddha had contact (for example, the meeting of eye, form and eye-consciousness), and feeling was there, but because he had attained true knowledge and eradicated ignorance, he did not have any craving linked to that feeling.

Vedanā nirodhā tanhā nirodho – with the cessation of feeling, craving ceases. *Tanhā nirodhā upādāna nirodho* – with the cessation of craving, clinging ceases. *Upādāna nirodhā, bhava nirodho* – with the cessation of clinging, the arranging of *kamma* ceases.

The Supreme Buddha had knowledge about this process from its beginning, so although the Supreme Buddha continued to teach Dhamma to others, to eat, to speak, and to think, there was not the arranging of *kamma*. That had ceased. With the cessation of the arranging of kamma, there would not be another birth. *Bhava nirodhā, jāti nirodho* – with the cessation of the arranging of *kamma*, birth ceases. *Jāti nirodhā, jarā-marana nirodho* – with the cessation of birth, aging and death cease.

"Nirodho, nirodho, ti kho bhikkhave! –"This is the cessation, this is the cessation!" "Pubbe ananussutesu dhammesu." – "This knowledge has never been attained before."

With that knowledge, the eye of Dhamma arose in the Supreme Buddha *(cakkum udapādi);* knowledge arose *(ñānam udapādi);* wisdom arose *(paññā udapādi);* true knowledge arose *(vijjā udapādi);* and *light arose (aloko udapādi).*

With this wisdom, he achieved the third kind of knowledge: *(āsavakkhaya ñāna) the knowledge of the destruction of all defilements.* Taints (or defilements) are the cause for birth. With the knowledge of the Four Noble Truths, the Supreme Buddha eradicated all taints and the roots of all taints.

He had now achieved three kinds of knowledge (knowledge of past lives, knowledge of the passing away and reappearing of beings, and knowledge of the destruction of all taints), and he was not a Bodhisatta any longer. During the full moon night, under the Bodhi Tree, in the same seat, without the help of a teacher, he became the Enlightened One. We go for refuge to our Great Teacher, the fully Enlightened One – Gautama Sammā Sambuddha.

Sādhu! Sādhu! Sādhu!

May you have the opportunity to understand the Four Noble Truths in Gautama Sammā Sambuddha's Dispensation.

↝ *Ānanda Sutta*
Leading to Awakening

SAMYUTTA NIKĀYA 54:13

Today we will discuss *ānāpānasati* meditation (meditation on in and out breathing). Ānanda Sutta is the name of this discourse, delivered by the Supreme Buddha.

With the Help of One Factor

Once, Venerable Ānanda questioned the Blessed One, *"Is there a factor, Blessed One, which when developed and pursued brings four factors to completion, and four factors which, when developed and pursued bring seven factors to completion, and seven factors which, when developed and pursued bring two noble factors to completion?"*

The Blessed One replied, *"Yes, Ānanda, there is one factor which, when developed and pursued brings four factors to completion. And there are four factors which, when developed and pursued bring seven factors to completion. And there are seven factors which, when developed and pursued bring two noble factors to completion."*

Then Venerable Ānanda asked, *"Blessed One, what is this one factor?"*

The Supreme Buddha explained to Venerable Ānanda, *"This one factor is **ānāpānasati**, which when developed and pursued brings **the four foundations of mindfulness** (cattāro satipatthāna) to completion. The four foundations of mindfulness, when developed and pursued bring **the seven factors of enlightenment** to completion. The seven factors of enlightenment, when developed and pursued bring **clear knowing and release** to completion."*

Concentrating and calming the mind by breathing in and breathing out, mindfully with full awareness, is known as *ānāpānasati*.

Then, what would be the four foundations of mindfulness? The *four foundations of mindfulness* are:

- *contemplation of the body,*
- *contemplation of feelings,*
- *contemplation of the mind, and*
- *contemplation of mental objects or thoughts.*

This fourfold mindfulness, when developed and pursued brings the seven factors of enlightenment *(satta bojjhanga)* to completion. *Satta bojjhanga* are the factors which fulfill the complete realization of the Dhamma.

There are two elements to this realization – *clear knowing (vijjā)* and *release (vimutti)*. Clear knowing is insight, and release is deliverance from defilements. Release or deliverance from defilements can be accomplished by comprehending the causes for defilements, through the development of one factor. This factor is *ānāpānasati*.

A Strong Foundation (Virtue – *Sīla*)

There is another thing that we should keep in mind. The four foundations of mindfulness cannot be realized through simple discussion. Some basic groundwork is needed. Can we build a massive building on a land without a strong foundation? No, we cannot. The building would collapse since there isn't a strong base. Likewise, in order to pursue the four foundations of mindfulness, it is essential to have a strong foundation.

The foundation is virtue or morality *(sīla)*. This is the discipline in speech, action and thought. Control of verbal and physical action is somewhat easy. The more difficult task is controlling the mind. Nevertheless, there is a technique for disciplining the mind. It is called the *restraint of faculties*.

First, a person would abstain from killing, stealing, sexual misconduct and taking liquor or drugs that cause intoxication. Now, he is controlled with respect to physical action. Then, he would abstain from false speech, divisive speech, abusive speech and idle chatter. Now, he has anchored himself in refraining from unskilful actions with both body and speech. The next step would be controlling of mind. Having developed the virtues that purify speech and action, cleansing his thoughts is now a less difficult task.

What would be the process he adopts for mental development? He would go about it in the following manner. We have five physical sense organs – eye, ear, nose, tongue and body. The awareness or consciousness comes through these sense organs. He begins by preventing the cultivation of unwholesome thoughts. Let's assume there is something that is unwholesome and blameworthy, yet we desire it very much. What should we do in this situation? We must be intelligent enough to think thus: *'Although I am enjoying this at this moment, it will bring painful consequences throughout samsāra'*. In this manner, with the understanding of the misery and suffering of endless *samsāra*, every effort must be made to prevent the arising of evil and unwholesome thoughts. This is the way to establish a solid base for developing the fourfold mindfulness.

This Mind has been Defiled for a Long Time

The word *meditation (bhāvanā)* is used so often that we believe it is something very easy to do. In our normal life when we study a subject, all we have to do is to listen, write and then memorize it. But, meditation is not an easy subject, as such. Meditation has to be viewed in the right context. Our minds are obsessed with facts and thoughts. Indeed, it is very difficult for us to turn away from habitual ways of thought and conduct.

We are well aware that many in this country practise meditation as a way to liberate from suffering. However, when investigated deeply, we find that they haven't made much progress. Therefore, it is clear that the practice of mindfulness is a difficult task. Mind is the core of our existence and for a long time it has been defiled. If we had purified and developed minds, it wouldn't be necessary for us to gather here today.

Firstly, we should understand that the mind is defiled by delusion and obsessed with all kinds of useless things. We have constructed our world either by seeing a visible object with the eye, hearing a sound with the ear, smelling an odour with the nose, tasting a flavour with the tongue, touching a tangible object with the body, or cognizing a mind-object with the mind.

If someone advises us to release ourselves from the world, (which has been constructed by the six-sense faculties), to a certain extent, we would see the benefit. Why is that? It is because we understand the misery of the world, with which we are engrossed. Therefore, we are aware that we should be liberated, and we strive for liberation from this misery.

Virtue *(sīla)* is the stepping stone. It is the foundation for mental development. For this purpose, the sense organs must be controlled. This is very important. If after reflecting on an object, unwholesome thoughts associated with desire, hatred and delusion arise in our minds, we should be fully aware of this. Then, we should consider the disadvantages of the unwholesome thoughts in this way: *'These thoughts of mind are unwholesome and bring painful consequences to me and others'*.

With determination, those unwholesome thoughts should then be removed. By the removal of evil and unwholesome thoughts, the mind stands firm and becomes calm. The Exalted One has expounded this repeatedly. It is essential for us to discipline ourselves and make a strong foundation before we undertake the difficult task of training our mind through meditation.

Prepare to Breathe Mindfully (Step 1)

We would start by going to a quiet place, away from the hustle and bustle of daily life. Keep in mind however, that although we may go to a quiet place, which is away from the rattle of busy life, the mind cannot be relaxed easily. We can find seclusion physically by going into a room and keeping it locked. But, would the mind be secluded? We must adjust our minds for seclusion and quiet contemplation.

The Exalted One expounded how mindfulness of in and out breathing *(ānāpānasati)* is developed and pursued so as to bring the four foundations of mindfulness to their culmination.

"Ānanda, there is the case where a monk, having gone to the wilderness, to the shade of a tree, or to an empty hut, sits down, and always mindful, he breathes in; mindful, he breathes out".

For this meditation one needs the sitting posture with a straightened upper body and legs crossed. The Blessed One always recommended this sitting posture for *ānāpānasati* meditation. The Blessed One had not advocated a sitting posture for any other type of meditation. However, a person who has gained mental development through *ānāpānasati* meditation, can then continue by maintaining any posture.

"Ujum kāyam panidhāya parimukham satim upatthapetvā" – *"Holding his body erect, he sets mindfulness on the body."*

Then, the normal breath should be noticed and observed. It is essential to be mindful of the breath. But, are we able to at once focus the mind on the breath and eliminate all other thoughts? No, it is difficult to do so. The mind wanders to other thoughts. This is the nature of the unrestrained body and mind. That is why it is essential to first discipline ourselves in speech and action. Then, we can train our mind for meditation.

If you have performed an unskilful action with your body and speech, your mind gets agitated and keeps on repenting the act. To avoid this, one should have a strong determination to preserve mindfulness, and never act *mindlessly*. If we entertain various kinds of distracting thoughts, we cannot train the mind to concentrate on the object of meditation. That is why the mental calm through virtue is important.

Contemplation of Body (I)
Pay Attention to Your Natural Breath (Step 2)

"So sato va assasati, sato va passasati"–
"Always mindful, he breathes in; mindful, he breathes out."

The in-breathing and out-breathing we know is automatic, and this happens throughout the day. However, when we try to breathe mindfully it is indeed complicated. Some people face difficulties in breathing when they try to breathe consciously, or mindfully. Some cannot notice the breath. The breath flows freely in its own natural rhythm; and normally, this flow of breath is not noticed. However, it is not easy to be mindful of the breath.

Start your meditation on mindfulness of in and out breathing with your eyes closed. Merely allow the breath to ebb and flow freely under the light of full awareness. Your one and only aim is to focus the mind on the breath. You should not try to find the point where the moving air strokes the nostrils, but keep your focus at the nose breath. Breathe in and breathe out mindfully with full awareness. Your breathing should be very natural and effortless.

Are you Ready to Accept the Challenge?

The Blessed One further explains:
"Dīgham va assasanto, dīgam assasāmi'ti pajānāti" –
"Breathing in long, he knows that he is breathing in long."

"Dīgham va passasanto, dīgham passasāmi'ti pajānāti" –
"Breathing out long, he knows that he is breathing out long."

How did he begin? He started breathing in and breathing out mindfully with full awareness. Now, he has gone a little further. Let's suppose, a beginner, while he is continuing the mindfulness practice in this manner, suddenly becomes overwhelmed with anger for some reason. What should he do? Should he suspend the meditation of mindfulness of in and out breathing and continue to nourish his anger? Mindfulness is observing whatever happens inside oneself. He should become aware that his mind is away from the primary meditation object. He is now aware of the obstacle that confronts him.

How is one's mind possessed by ill will and anger? The anger will be there as long as it is willingly received and nourished. So, how would we overcome this obstacle? We should clearly understand that it is only *'a concept'*. The meditator should put forth his will to overcome the anger by wishing for the welfare and happiness of all beings. Then, the vicious thoughts of hatred will be forgotten.

Similarly, when sensual desire or passion is present in him, he should reflect upon the repulsiveness of the body and establish thinking in this way: *'Indeed this body is full of impurities and one day it will disintegrate into dust.'* By seeing and being mindful on the repulsive nature of the body, he can detach from sensual desire and overcome this obstacle.

Now, bring your attention back to the primary object – breathing. Breathe in and breathe out mindfully with full awareness. This may only be for a short while, and again your mind may become distracted. It may wander and you may find it difficult to concentrate. For example, if you have travelled extensively around the world, your mind may start strolling all over the world! Whenever your mind wanders to other thoughts, be aware of them. One needs a lot of effort to manage these distractions and focus on the real task of maintaining concentration. You should not try to strain your body, as it is the mental effort that should be strong and effective.

We should strive with diligence to train the mind, but this must be done sensitively. Suppose there is a greasy object floating in the water. What would happen if one tried to grasp it by squeezing the object? It would slip through the fingers. But if you were to catch it gently and mindfully, you would be more likely to succeed.

Mental training is also something that should be done carefully and patiently. It is through gradual training that one can observe the mind and control it. What are the prerequisites for this? Firstly, effort is required, and then, the awareness and the ability to understand. Someone may sit for many hours keeping the body motionless, but no one would really know what he is thinking.

Blocking the Entry

The Exalted One pointed out that when the meditator is mindful and attentive with breathing meditation, he is fully aware of the differences in the rhythm of his breathing. *Breathing in long, he knows that he is breathing in long; breathing out long, he knows that he is breathing out long.* He is gradually gaining the power of concentration and his mind does not wander to other thoughts. The stress and tension of his body and mind are starting to ease. His concentration is high, and with it, comes rapturous joy, calm, and peace of mind.

For some, when they become relieved like this, they cling to this joy viewing it as *'I'* or *'my self'*. Why does this happen? In this life process we hold the wrong view of personality-belief; belief in a *'self'*. Let's suppose, with this personality-belief, a person meditates for a few hours, and he is very happy and relieved to have meditated successfully. The next time he sits for meditation, he sits with a new problem in mind, which he did not have earlier. What is this problem? The first time, he managed to gain concentration by focusing the mind. This time, he expects to regain that concentration as soon as he sits down to meditate. Therefore, this time he sits with a new expectation – one which he did not have the first time. Previously, he gained concentration by focusing his mind on one solitary object, to the exclusion of all others. This time, his mind is in a hurry to experience the same concentration again, and this eagerness scatters his mind.

A gentleman here asked a question on whether one could shut himself off from anger or desire if they arise during meditation. Yes, for some, it is possible. As it comes in, whatever the object, you will make note of it, and then shut yourself off from it altogether. How do you do this successfully?

For one person, life is like a house with six doors, but he keeps only one door open. He then has the ability to identify everyone who enters and exits through this door, and also block the entry of unwanted persons. Another person may keep all six doors open, and stand at one door. In this case, anybody can walk in and out through the other doors.

The ability to maintain one-pointedness of the mind (without being distracted) will depend on the nature of each person. That is, how many doors they habitually keep open, and their ability to keep only one door open.

Identifying Long and Short Breathing – Like a Skilful Carpenter (Step 3)

The Exalted One explained long and short breath with a simile. Just as a skilful carpenter, while making a long turn, understands clearly, *'I am making a long turn.'*, the meditator when breathing in long, he knows that he is breathing in long; and when breathing out long, he knows that he is breathing out long. Or, breathing in short, he knows that he is breathing in short; and breathing out short, he knows that he is breathing out short.

What made him notice and understand this difference? As he continues developing the various degrees of mindfulness, his mind gets fully concentrated on the breath. At times the breath may become so subtle that one can hardly catch it. You must be skilful enough to become aware of the breath again.

Experiencing the Whole Body of Breath, He Trains (Step 4)

"Sabba kāya patisamvedī assasissāmī'ti sikkhati,
Sabba kāya patisamvedī passasissāmī'ti sikkkhati."

The Blessed One expounded thus: *"Experiencing the whole body I shall breathe in; experiencing the whole body, I shall breathe out'. Thus, he trains himself."*

One can be mindful of the breath and not of the body. He can do so when his mind is fully concentrated only on the breath. Yet, it is like another body as mentioned in the Dhamma. Here, he trains himself to breathe in sensitive to the entire body of the breath, and to breathe out sensitive to the entire body of the breath.

Calming the In and Out Breath, He Trains (Step 5)

"Passambhayam kāya sankhāram assasissāmī'ti sikkhati.
Passambhayam kāya sankhāram passasissāmī 'ti sikkhati."

Here, the meditator trains himself to *breathe in, calming the bodily process (kāyasankhāra – in and out breath), and to breathe out, calming the bodily process.* With the calmness of the entire process – body and mind, he begins to experience rapture.

Contemplation of Feelings (II)
Experiencing Rapture, He Trains (Step 6)
Experiencing Joy, He Trains (Step 7)

"Pīti patisamvedī assasissāmī'ti sikkhati,
Pīti patisamvedī passasissāmī'ti sikkhati."

Now he is fully concentrated on the breath. His concentration is very high. Rapturous joy, calm, and peace of mind are incredible experiences for him – something he has not experienced before. Remember, he is training himself. Therefore, he does not cling to this rapturous joy. He trains himself to *breathe in experiencing rapture*, and to *breathe out experiencing rapture*. He continues this in a calm detached way.

Some people become elated when they get the feeling of happiness and bliss to the body and mind. A mind that is obsessed by elation cannot concentrate. At that point, the concentration he gained would disappear. Then he starts regretting as to why he could not uphold the concentration he developed previously. Concentration, rapturous joy, calm, and peace of mind and body, are causally dependent; they are conditioned results. They do not arise by chance. If the mind is *self*, there wouldn't be a problem. As it would be possible to say with regards to the mind, *'Let my mind be thus.'* However, mind is not *self*.

Now he trains himself to *breathe in sensitive to rapture*, and to *breathe out sensitive to rapture*. Calming the entire process of body and mind, he is experiencing rapture. He is experiencing this as a result of **continuous exertion for deliverance from mental defilements** (*ātāpi*) and from **clear comprehension** (*sampajāno*).

Is the rapture easeful or stressful? It is indeed easeful – physically and mentally. He is breathing in sensitive to pleasure and breathing out sensitive to pleasure, experiencing bliss. You can understand to what extent he has tamed his mind. The common nature of the mind is that it can be swayed by anything. He has trained himself and therefore, his mind is not being mesmerized by pleasure and rapture. His mind is tamed, controlled and restrained with continuous exertion for deliverance from defilements. His mind is fully concentrated on the breath, and his concentration is very high. What will he do next?

He Trains Experiencing the Mental Formations (Step 8)

"Citta sankhāra patisamvedī assasissāmī'ti sikkhati.
Citta sankhāra patisamvedī passasissāmī'ti sikkhati."

'Experiencing the mental formations, he breathes in. Experiencing the mental formations, he breathes out. Thus, he trains himself.'

What are these mental formations *(citta sankhāra)*? These mental formations are two recognizable attributes – *perception and feeling (saññā* and *vedanā)*. **Feeling** is noted as pleasant, unpleasant and neutral. Here, it is a pleasant feeling, both physically and mentally. **Perception** is the recognition of objects. In this case, he perceives the status he gained with the development of mindfulness of in and out breathing. Experiencing the rapturous joy – physically and mentally, he trains himself *to breathe in experiencing mental formations, and to breathe out experiencing mental formations.*

Calming Mental Formations, He Trains (Step 9)

The Exalted One explained how one can further develop and pursue mindfulness of in and out breathing, thus:

"Passambhayam citta sankhāram assasissāmī'ti sikkhati.
Passambhayam citta sankhāram passasissāmī'ti sikkhati."

"Calming mental formations, he breathes in. Calming mental formations, he breathes out. Thus, he trains himself."

Earlier he trained himself to breathe in and out sensitive to rapture and pleasure. You may understand the degree to which his mind is being tamed now. Within what he *feels and perceives*, without getting obsessed by rapture and joy, he trains himself to breathe in and out, *calming mental formations*. Now what happens?

"Vedanāsu vedananupassī tasmim samaye bhikkhu viharati."
"On that occasion, the monk lives contemplating feelings in feelings."

By now, he has developed his awareness to such an extent where he dwells *contemplating feelings (vedanānupassana),* within the mindfulness of in and out breathing. *Ānāpānasati* (mindfulness of in and out breathing) is a form of *kāyānupassana* (contemplation of the body). Thus, the meditator is now developing the contemplation of feelings *(vedanānupassana)* within the contemplation of the body *(kāyānupassana).*

What is contemplation of feelings? **Contemplation of feelings** is becoming mindful of feelings as pleasant, unpleasant or neutral. He remains mindfully and ardently focused on feelings, in and of themselves.

Here, it does not mean *'amisa vedanā' – feeling, which is related to the world of sensual pleasures,* such as pleasant, unpleasant or neutral feelings that one experiences when seeing a visible object, hearing a sound, smelling an odour, tasting a flavour or touching something tangible. The feeling he is experiencing here is a *sensation related to the higher meditational realms (nirāmisa vedanā).*

We should not forget that our discussion is based on the mindfulness of in and out breathing *(ānāpānasati bhāvanā).* The four foundations of mindfulness *(cattāro satipatthāna)* are explained well in the Supreme Buddha's Teachings, the Noble Dhamma. However, in many places within Sri Lanka where meditation is being taught, the instructors do not teach this as explained in the Dhamma. While in the process of breathing in and out, they instruct meditators that if they should feel a pain in some part of the body, let's say the knee, meditators should switch all of their mental energy to their knee and note in the mind as "pain, pain". But that is not the correct interpretation. What is clearly specified is how contemplation of feelings *(vedanānupassana)* is developed by mindfulness of in and out breathing *(ānāpānasati)*.

In Supreme Buddha's Dhamma, it is clearly explained how mindfulness of in and out breathing is developed and pursued so as to bring the four foundations of mindfulness to their culmination. When first developing mindfulness of in and out breathing, the meditator discerns the differences of his breathing, and remains focused on the breath. This is *kāyānupassana*. Thereafter, he discerns the differences of the mind as he trains himself to breathe in and out sensitive to rapture and pleasure. Thus, he is experiencing feeling and perception. Further, perceiving the differences (of feeling and perception in his mind), he trains himself to breathe in and out calming mental formations. At that point, he remains focused on feelings *(vedanānupassana)* – ardent, alert, and mindful, with continuous exertion for deliverance, restraining greed and distress.

This is how mindfulness of in and out breathing brings the contemplation of body and contemplation of feeling to their culmination.

It is now obvious that this meditation needs to be developed and pursued ardently with thorough understanding and awareness. One should realize how strong and enormous the mental effort and patience need to be, in order to bring about mental purity and perfection.

There is one more thing to remember. Not everyone can develop *ānāpānasati bhāvanā* immediately. Once, Venerable Rāhula, as a young novice, approached Arahant Sāriputta, and was advised to develop and pursue *ānāpānasati*. At the time, Venerable Rāhula did not know the way to develop *ānāpānasati*, and so, he went to the Blessed One and asked, *"Would the Blessed One teach me about ānāpānasati?"*

The Blessed One, when exhorting the novice Venerable Rāhula, first gave detailed instructions on *vipassana* – a method to investigate with insight, by analyzing aggregates, material elements, sense spheres, etc..., and then finally instructed him on the practice of *ānāpānasati* meditation. The reason is that the Blessed One recognized Venerable Rāhula's temperament and what would be most suitable for him. Could we all be cured from our various illnesses by using one type of medicine? No, we could not. Different medicines are being prescribed for different types of ailments, depending on each individual's physical condition. Likewise, as temperaments differ, so do the objects of meditation.

Supreme Buddha taught many ways to meditate. The Blessed One taught *ānāpānasati* to those with the ability to keep mindfulness well. The Supreme Buddha was emphatic on the importance of practising *ānāpānasati*, and described it as peaceful, sublime, and perfects the four foundations of mindfulness. However, if one continually tries but cannot establish mindfulness on breathing, then he can practise other kinds of meditation for the time being.

"Vedanaññatarāham Ānanda etam vadami,
Yadidam assāsa – passāsānam sādhukam manasikāram."

"Ānanda, when I say, 'by proper attention to inhalation-exhalation', it is like another feeling."

Most of the meditation practices that have become popular today are not in line with the Dhamma. Those practices are to note in your mind, "pain, pain", when you feel pain in some part of your body during meditation, and this they say is *vedanānupassana* – contemplation on feeling. If your mind goes somewhere, they say to note "going, going", and this they say is *cittānupassana* – the contemplation of mind. If you feel sleepy, they say to note "sleepy, sleepy". And, if a desire or agitation presents itself in the mind, they say to note "desire, desire", or "agitation, agitation", and this they say is *dhammānupassana* – the contemplation of mind objects. Those are the incorrect practices today that people are being taught as meditation.

However, the futility of such practices is apparent when studying the word of the Tathāgata: *"I say, 'practising ānāpānasati, by paying attention to experience these (rapture, pleasure, feeling, perception) is said to be a certain kind of feeling'."*

Contemplation of Mind (III)
Experiencing the Highly Concentrated Mind (Step 10)

The Blessed One explains thereafter:

"Citta patisamvedī assasissāmi'ti sikkhati.
Citta patisamvedī passasissāmi'ti sikkhati."

"Experiencing the mind, he breathes in. Experiencing the mind, he breathes out. Thus he trains himself."

He trained himself to breathe in sensitive to pleasure, and to breathe out sensitive to pleasure. Now, what is he developing successively? He is developing equanimity – the result of a calm concentrated mind. He is able to do this because he did not get attached to that pleasure in the mind. He cognized all differences that occurred in the mind (perceptions of in and out breathing, rapture, pleasure, etc...). He experienced the mental formations – feeling and perception in *ānāpānasati*, without being swayed by them. He is now very sensitive to the mind. Experiencing the highly concentrated mind, that is inclined to equanimity, he breathes in and breathes out. Thus, he trains himself.

Gladdening the Mind, He Trains (Step 11)

He further trains himself:
"Abhippamodayam cittam assasissāmī'ti sikkhati.
Abhippamodayam cittam passasissāmī'ti sikkhati."

"Gladdening the mind, he breathes in. Gladdening the mind, he breathes out. Thus, he trains himself."

Without clinging to the gladdening of the mind by calming; without being scattered; and without being obsessed by sense desire, ill will or sloth and torpor, he trains himself.

Gladdening the mind is described as peaceful, pure happiness. This satisfaction occurs in a mind that is well guarded and restrained; in a mind that is not obsessed by the five hindrances. Such a mind indeed, brings great bliss. He is not confused or puzzled. He trains himself to breathe in and breathe out, increasingly gladdening the mind.

Thoroughly Establishing Mindfulness, He Trains (Step 12)

"Samādaham cittam assasissāmī'ti sikkhati.
Samādaham cittam passasissāmī'ti sikkhati."

"Concentrating the mind, he breathes in. Concentrating the mind, he breathes out. Thus he trains himself."

Now he trains himself to breathe in and breathe out, thoroughly establishing mindfulness. His mind is fully concentrated.

Releasing the Mind from Hindrances (Step 13)

"Vimocayam cittam assasissāmī'ti sikkhati.
Vimocayam cittam passasissāmī'ti sikkhati."

"Liberating the mind, he breathes in. Liberating the mind, he breathes out. Thus he trains himself."

Now he is liberating the mind from the *nivarana* or *hindrances* (sensual desire, ill will, sloth and torpor, restlessness, drowsiness and doubt). He trains himself to breathe in and to breathe out releasing the mind. What is he developing now?

"Citte cittānupassī bhikkhu tasmim samaye viharati."

"Ānanda, on that occasion the monk remains focused on the mind in and of itself – ardent, alert and mindful. His mindfulness of in and out breathing is developed and pursued so as to bring the contemplation of mind (cittānupassana) to its culmination."

With Ardent, Clear Comprehension and Mindfulness

Now, let's review this progress from the beginning. First he trained himself to breathe in and out experiencing the body. This is *kāyānupassana* (contemplation of the body).

"Kāye kāyānupassī Ānanda bhikkhu tasmim samaye viharati."

The Exalted One expounded: *"Ānanda, on that occasion the monk remains focused on the body, in and of itself."*

The Blessed One regularly repeated the phrase, *"Ātāpi – sampajāno satimā vineyya loke abijjha domanassam."* The completion of the four foundations of mindfulness *(cattāro satipatthāna)* within the concentration of *ānāpānasati*, cannot be considered as a given. *Satipatthāna* means the setting up of mindfulness. Establishing or setting up of mindfulness cannot be done effortlessly. As explained above, there are certain requirements that need to be fulfilled in establishing mindfulness.

Ātāpi is *ardent and continuous exertion and perseverance for the development of concentration and deliverance from defilements.*

Sampajāna means *clear comprehension for deliverance from defilements, wrong views and perceptions.*

Satimā is *mindfulness to focus the mind on the ānāpānasati,* to the exclusion of all other thoughts and to fix the mind there.

What is *vineyya loke abijjha domanassam*? Eye, ear, nose, tongue, body and mind are the world. The world as experienced from these faculties, is continually correlating with the world of form, sound, smell, taste, tangibles, and mental objects. Interaction with the external world normally creates defilements like greed and distress. Therefore, we must tame and restrain this greed and distress, as described previously.

With the development of *kāyānupassana* he was in a position to bring *vedanānupassana* to its culmination. By concentrating on *ānāpānasati* to a higher degree, he brings the *cittānupassana* to its culmination. He will now develop *dhammānupassana* *(contemplation of mind objects)*.

Purely based on the deep concentration of mind through mindfulness of in and out breathing, the meditator directs his thoughts to insight for the achievement of the noble goal. In view of this, the Blessed One exhorted thus:

"Nāham, Ānanda, mutthassatissa asampajānassa ānāpāna sati samadhi bhāvanam vadāmi." – *"I say, Ānanda, one who is inattentive, and who lacks clear comprehension, he is not one doing ānāpāna."*

Mind development achieved with great effort is not something that can be achieved overnight. It needs time and regular practice. Meditation is not only *ānāpānasati*. Reflection on the repulsive nature of the body is also a type of meditation. Some people find it difficult to concentrate on mindfulness of in and out breathing, but they might be able to develop the meditation on repulsiveness *(asubha)*. Some can very well develop the meditation on loving kindness *(mettā)*, and others can develop the concentration of reflection on material elements *(dhātumanasikāra)*. As temperaments differ, so do the objects of meditation.

Those who can practise mindfulness to a high degree, can get fully concentrated on the *ānāpānasati*. They can frequently practise and develop *ānāpānasati*. If a person who has developed the concentration of mindfulness on *ānāpānasati* inquires from another person about his development on *ānāpānasati*, that person may reply, '*Oh no, I cannot develop concentration at all!*' In case you come across a person who is unable to develop concentration of mindfulness on *ānāpānasati*, you should not criticize him under any circumstances. You only have to encourage him to select another object of meditation that is more suitable for him.

We cannot properly analyze ourselves without first *practising* a meditation. We cannot judge the mind even after meditating for one or two hours. Some cannot develop concentration even if they practise throughout the entire day. However, if you continue to practise *ānāpānasati* with strong determination for a few days, concentration could develop gradually. Therefore, you should not get disheartened for not obtaining a significant achievement by practising just for a few hours.

Let's suppose a person goes to a lonely place and tries to practise *ānāpānasati* for just a few minutes. He is in a hurry, and so when he is not successful in *ānāpānasati*, he switches over to meditation on loving kindness (*mettā*). And again, after a little while, he finds it impossible to continue, so he changes the meditation object and starts meditation on the extraordinary qualities of the Supreme Buddha (*Buddhānussati*). Following that, he is not mindful or patient, and switches to practising walking-meditation. Finally, without practising anything properly, he gives up altogether. You cannot practise mindfulness in this manner. You should strive hard to train your mind and develop the best that is in you. For some, it is easier. They have determination and persistence as ingrained qualities, and they are less likely to get discouraged.

The Exalted One made clear how one can train himself to breathe in and out, liberating the mind from the five hindrances. Now, his mindfulness is fully developed, his concentration is very strong, his mindfulness is thoroughly established, and his mental effort is enduring. Having gained perfect and concentrative calm, he is now able to develop insight *(vipassanā)* meditation – to see reality.

Contemplation of Mind Objects (IV)
Contemplating on Impermanence, He Trains (Step 14)

The Blessed One explains:

"Aniccānupassī assasissāmī'ti sikkhati.
Aniccānupassī passasissāmī'ti sikkhati."

"Contemplating impermanence, he breathes in. Contemplating impermanence, he breathes out. Thus, he trains himself."

Anicca means *'impermanence'*. Being able to see everything in terms of impermanence is not something that comes automatically after gaining concentration of mind. Now, he trains himself to *breathe in contemplating impermanence,* and he trains himself to *breathe out contemplating impermanence.*

Some meditation teachers declare that impermanence is something that just becomes visible to a mind, like appearing in a meter, and enables one to gain something called *'vipassana nana'* *(insight knowledge)* by continuous determination. This theory or view is not in accordance with the Supreme Buddha's Dhamma.

Impermanence of Breath

Ānāpānasati is something that should be developed and pursued mindfully and discerningly. Now, he trains himself to breathe in focusing on impermanence, and to breathe out focusing on impermanence. Purity of mind has been achieved through the elimination of the hindrances *(nīvarana).* His effort, mindfulness and concentration are now being directed towards focusing on impermanence. He is contemplating on impermanence within *ānāpānasati.* He can see the impermanent nature of his own breath in its rise and fall; the impermanence of his body; and the impermanent nature of the pleasant feeling and perception that he experienced.

Impermanence of Body

What has he seen in the body? What does this body consist of? This physical body contains and comprises the four great elements, which are known as: solidity/earth *(pathavi)*, fluidity/water *(āpo)*, heat or temperature *(tejo)* and air *(vāyo)*. We generally use the word *rūpa* (material form) to denote the body. When he is breathing in and out, he is focusing on impermanence of material form which is derived from the four great elements.

Impermanence of Feeling

Thereafter, he is focusing on feelings. *Dependent on contact, feeling arises.* What is contact? Contact is the coming together of three things. For example, eye, form and eye-consciousness come together, and it is their convergence, that is called *contact*. Similarly, with ear and sounds, nose and smells, and so on, through to mind and mental-objects.

In this instance, when body, tangible object and consciousness come together, there arises contact. With the arising of contact, simultaneously, there arises feeling *(vedanā)* – feeling born of body contact. Since feeling is conditioned by contact, feeling differs in accordance with the change of contact. This way, he contemplates on the impermanence of feeling.

Impermanence of Perception

Then, there is the recognition of perception. This is called *saññā* (*perception*) which is also subject to change as it is conditioned by contact. Perception changes due to impermanence of contact.

Impermanence of Formations

Perception is followed by *sankhāra* (mental formations). If the mental factor was directed to a certain matter, on that occasion there is volitional activity, and this is called *sankhāra*. Here, he observes the impermanence of the mental formation with the change of contact. All these are based on the activities of the mind.

Now he understands every aspect in this life process which was considered as *self* (form, feeling, perception and formation); or *anything pertaining to a self*. He has real wisdom to see things as they really are. One may contemplate on impermanence saying *"anicca, anicca"* continuously, but still be holding onto the notion of *"I am"* or *"mine"*. To avoid this, it is important to realize the *impermanent, no-self* nature in inhalation-exhalation and in any other external object.

Impermanence of Consciousness

Finally, he sees the impermanent nature of all that has been cognized (the rise and fall of breath, rapture, joy, feelings, and perceptions). It is through this insight that the true nature of ***the five aggregates of clinging*** is understood and seen in the light of impermanence:

- ***material form*** *(rūpa)* derived from the four great elements,
- ***feeling*** *(vedanā)* that is conditioned by contact,
- ***perception*** *(saññā)* that is conditioned by contact,

- *mental formations (sankhāra)* that is conditioned by contact, and
- *consciousness (viññāna)* that is conditioned by mentality-materiality *(nāma-rūpa)*

Being fully concentrated on *ānāpānasati*, he now dwells ardent, with full awareness, and clear comprehension of impermanence. With the base of this awareness, established in *anicca (impermanence)*, he develops an understanding of his own life, the impermanent nature of others who breathe and live, and the impermanent nature of material form, feeling, perception, mental formations and consciousness (the five aggregates of clinging).

Thus, he observes the impermanent characteristic of phenomenal existence, internally and externally. He does not see a difference in him and the outer world. He sees the characteristic of phenomenal existence as subject to *cause and effect*. Now he is gaining knowledge, and his comprehension is increasing. He sees *things as they really are*, in whatever material form: whether past, present or future, far or near, external or internal. He sees the impermanence even of the rapture and pleasure that he is experiencing in breathing mindfully. Now, based on the impermanent breath, he understands the impermanent nature of the five aggregates of clinging.

He realizes that whatever is impermanent and subject to change, is suffering *(dukkha)*. And, whatever is impermanent is *without self (anatta)*. It is through this insight that the true nature of the aggregates is clearly seen; in the light of three signs *(ti-lakkhana)*: *impermanence* **(anicca)**, *suffering* **(dukkha)** and *without self* **(anatta)**.

He sees the impermanent, suffering and *no-self* nature of all conditioned and component things. As a result, he knows there is no *"I"*, no *self*, or *anything pertaining to a self*. When he trains himself to breathe in and out focusing on impermanence, he understands that anything taken as *'mine'* is impermanent; anything taken as *'I am'* is impermanent; and anything that is taken as *'my self'* is impermanent. He realizes that whatever is impermanent, is *without self.* That which is *without self,* is not *'mine',* not *'I am',* and is not *'my self'.* Thus he sees everything as it really is – with wisdom.

Contemplating Detachment, He Trains (Step 15)

"Virāgānupassī assasissāmī'ti sikkhati.
Virāganupassī passasissāmī'ti sikkhati."

"Contemplating detachment he breathes in, contemplating detachment he breathes out. Thus, he trains himself."

With this realization, he understands clearly that what is impermanent is not worth clinging to. If his mind was obsessed by the five hindrances, he would not be able to concentrate successfully on an object of a wholesome nature, and he would not be able to avoid clinging.

But here, he has tamed and guarded his mind very well by training himself to breathe in and out, focusing on impermanence. With that development, he now trains himself to focus on dispassion. Thus, he becomes dispassionate towards: material form, feeling, perception, mental formations and consciousness. He becomes dispassionate towards the five aggregates of clinging by seeing the true nature. This is not a kind of disinterest or simple boredom. This is a *true realization.* With this awareness as a foundation, he develops an understanding of his own life.

Through dispassion, he is detached from material form, detached from feeling, detached from perception, detached from mental formations, and detached from consciousness. Now, he is breathing in and out with the view of *no-self*. He sees the arising and passing away of the five aggregates of clinging. He neither makes any identification, nor has any attachment towards *'I'*, *'me'* or *'mine'*. Observing the phenomenon of arising and passing, he develops *wisdom* which leads to *detachment*.

He trains himself to *breathe in focusing on dispassion*, and to *breathe out focusing on dispassion*. In this way, he dwells detached – without clinging towards anything in the world; without clinging to the body; without clinging to the pleasure he is experiencing in breathing; without clinging to perception; without clinging to the mental formations; and without clinging to consciousness.

Contemplating Cessation, He Trains (Step 16)

Now, he focuses on cessation. It is the cessation of what? It is not the cessation of material form, feeling, perception, mental formations or consciousness. It is the cessation of *the wrong view of personality-belief*, which he held with regards to the five aggregates of clinging, as this is *'mine'*, this *'I am'*, and this is *'my self'*. He understands the non-substantial *(non-self)* nature of the five aggregates of clinging.

Through developed insight, ignorance is abandoned. With the abandonment of ignorance, craving is eradicated. Craving is attachment, and attachment is abandoned. Desire and passion are abandoned. He is liberated. Yes, he is liberated from suffering!

Thus the Tathāgata explained to us:

"Nirodhānupassī assasissāmī'ti sikkhati.
Nirodhānupassī passasissāmī'ti sikkhati."

"Contemplating cessation, he breathes in. Contemplating cessation, he breathes out. Thus, he trains himself."

It is now clear how one comprehends, in their entirety, the Four Noble Truths. Suffering is the phenonmenal existence of the five aggregates of clinging. The cause for the arising of suffering is *craving*. Craving results from delusion, which prevents man from seeing things as they really are. Therefore, *cessation of suffering* is achieved when craving is eradicated and extinguished. The path leading to the cessation of craving is the Noble Eightfold Path, expounded by the Enlightened One.

The Supreme Buddha explained that the meditator trains to *breathe in focusing on cessation of craving*, and *to breathe out focusing on cessation of craving*.

Contemplating Relinquishment, He Trains (Step 17)

He now experiences relinquishment. He relinquishes lust, hatred and delusion, and he relinquishes the notion of 'I', 'me' or 'mine'. Thus, The Blessed One expounded that this one factor – *ānāpānasati*, when developed and pursued brings *clear knowing and release* to completion.

"Dhammesu dhammānupassī Ānanda tasmim samaye bhikkhu viharati." – *"On that occasion, Ānanda, the monk remains focused on mental qualities in and of themselves."*

Clear and Radiant, like the Sun and Moon

You can see the clarity of the path to *Nibbāna*. It is clear and radiant, like the sun and the moon. The meditator, the inquiring mind, will not find it difficult to understand this state. The Enlightened One has very distinctly explained how mindfulness of in and out breathing is developed and pursued so as to bring the four foundations of mindfulness to their culmination.

Does it say anything here so as to note "sleepy, sleepy" if you feel sleepy; or if a desire presents itself in the mind, to note "desire, desire" etc. No, it does not. *Ānāpānasati* meditation is indeed a discerning process that has to be followed carefully - as Supreme Buddha had instructed.

The Exalted One has pointed out so clearly how a meditator develops and pursues *ānāpānasati* to bring the four foundations of mindfulness to completion. He developed and pursued *ānāpānasati* with great effort and continuous exertion for deliverance from defilement *(ātāpī)*; with clear comprehension for deliverance from defilement *(sampajāno)*; with mindfulness *(satima)*; subduing greed and distress *(so yam tam hoti abhijjhā domanassānam pahānam)*, and clearly perceiving reality through discernment *(tam paññāya disvā)*. He is more and more equanimous *(sādhukam ajjhupekkhitā hoti)*.

This one factor, *ānāpānasati*, has been developed and pursued to bring the four foundations of mindfulness *(cattāro satipatthāna)* to completion.

Completion of the Seven Factors of Enlightenment

The Enlightened One further explains:
"Katam bhāvitā ca Ānanda katam bahulī katā satta bojjhange paripūrenti." – *"And Ānanda, how are the four foundations of mindfulness developed and pursued to bring the seven factors of enlightenment to their culmination?"*

Now, the seven factors of enlightenment *(satta bojjhanga)* should be cultivated in the mind. The Pāli term *'bojjhanga'* is composed of *bodhi* and *anga*. *'Bodhi'* is *the realization of the Four Noble Truths and 'anga' means 'conducing factors'*.

The *seven factors of enlightenment* are:

- *mindfulness (sati)*
- *analysis of the Dhamma (dhammavicaya)*
- *energy (vīriya)*
- *rapture (pīti)*
- *tranquility (passaddhi)*
- *concentration (samādhi)*
- *equanimity (upekkhā)*

Mindfulness is Steady

The mind is now well established on the four foundations of mindfulness, and highly concentrated on *ānāpānasati*.

"Tasmim samaye Ānanda bhikkhuno upatthitā sati hoti asammutthā." –
"Ānanda, on that occasion his mindfulness is steady and without lapse."

When he is breathing in and breathing out, focusing on impermanence, mindfulness as a factor of enlightenment, is aroused.

"Sati sambojjhango tasmim samaye bhikkhuno āraddho hoti."

On that occasion, he develops mindfulness as a factor of enlightenment.

The following terms are used by the Blessed One to describe *'bojjhanga' (factor of enlightenment)*:

- *viveka nissitam* – dependent on seclusion, gained by removing the five hindrances that defile the mind

- *virāga nissitam* – dependent on dispassion, gained from contemplating impermanence
- *nirodha nissitam* – dependent on the entire cessation of craving, and
- *vossagga parināmi* – resulting in relinquishment, leading to *Nibbāna*.

In this way, *mindfulness* becomes a factor of enlightenment.

Analyzing

"So tathā sato viharanto tam dhammam paññāya pavicinati pavicarati parivīmamsamāpajjati."

Remaining mindful in this way, he examines and analyzes the true nature of the five aggregates of clinging that are impermanent, unsatisfactory and *without self*. What is this doctrine? This is the doctrine of **conditionality**.

"Dhammavicaya sambojjhango tasmim samaye bhikkhuno āraddho hoti."

When he remains mindful in this way, examining, analyzing and coming to an understanding of the impermanence of the five aggregates of clinging, then, *analysis of the Dhamma* as a factor of enlightenment is aroused.

Great Effort

"Āraddham hoti viriyam asallīnam" –*"Exertion and increasing effort to strive and continue."*

When he examines and analyzes with discernment, persistent energy is aroused. The function of energy is to discard unwholesomeness that has arisen in the mind; to prevent the development of unwholesomeness that has not yet arisen; to develop wholesomeness that has not yet arisen; and to maintain and promote the further growth of wholesomeness that has already arisen, through meditation. *Energy* as a factor of enlightenment, is aroused.

With Rapture

As he proceeds with mindfulness, clear comprehension, persistent energy, and by seeing with insight, there arises intense joy. This joy or *rapture*, as a factor of enlightenment, is aroused.

Calm and Tranquil

"Kāyopi passambhati, cittampi passambhati."

When he is enraptured, the body becomes calm, and the mind becomes calm. When the body and mind of an enraptured monk becomes calm, then *tranquility*, as a factor of enlightenment, is aroused.

Mind Becomes Concentrated

"Yasmim samaye Ānanda bhikkhuno passaddha kāyassa sukhino cittam samādhiyati." – *"Ānanda, for one who is at ease – his body calmed, the mind becomes concentrated."*

Then, *concentration* as a factor of enlightenment, is aroused.

Equanimity

"Tathā samāhitam cittam sādhukam ajjhupekkhitā hoti." –*"He oversees the mind thus concentrated, with equanimity."*

Throughout all of this, he sees the five aggregates of clinging and the impermanent, unsatisfactory and *no-self* nature of the five aggregates of clinging. Therefore, he remains equanimous, alert and mindful. In this way, *equanimity* as a factor of enlightenment, is aroused.

From the foregoing, it is clear now that based on the four foundations of mindfulness – *kāyānupassana, vedanānupassana, cittānupassana* and *dhammānupassana*, the seven factors of enlightenment – *sati, dhammavicaya, vīriya, pīti, passadhi, samādhi* and *upekkhā* come to completion.

Therefore, mindfulness of in and out breathing – *ānāpānasati*, when developed and pursued, brings the four foundations of mindfulness to completion. And, the four foundations of mindfulness, when developed and pursued, bring the seven factors of enlightenment to completion.

Vijjā – Complete Knowledge of the Four Noble Truths *Vimutti* – Liberation from Craving

"Vijjā vimuttim paripūrenti." – *"The factors of enlightenment, when developed and pursued, bring clear knowing and release to completion."*

Clear knowing is the insight, and **release** is the liberation from threefold craving: *sensual craving (kāma-tanhā), craving for existence (bhava-tanhā),* and *craving for non-existence (vibhava-tanhā).*

This is the knowledge of reality – *seeing things as they really are,* and it is called *'yathābhuta ñana'*. By virtue of this clear knowing, he is liberated.

What is it that he previously did not see in its true nature? He did not see the *true nature of the five aggregates of clinging*. What is it that he sees now in its true nature? He sees the true nature of the five aggregates of clinging. Because of this, he has eradicated the *craving towards the five aggregates of clinging*. Through developed insight, *ignorance and craving are abandoned*.

He progressively discerned the impermanent, unsatisfactory and *non-self* nature of the five aggregates of clinging. He understands that all phenomenal existence is causally dependent *(paticca-samuppāda – dependent arising)*.

He released himself from *personality-belief (sakkāya ditthi)* – the wrong view of the five aggregates of clinging as permanent, satisfactory and *self*. He realized that there is no *"I"*, no persisting psychic entity, no ego principle, no *self*, or *anything pertaining to* a *self*.

True Deliverance by the Excellent Guidance of the Tathāgata

As expounded by the Tathāgata, *ānāpānasati*, when developed and pursued, brings the four foundations of mindfulness to completion. The four foundations of mindfulness when developed and pursued bring the seven factors of enlightenment to completion. The seven factors of enlightenment, when developed and pursued bring clear knowing and release to completion, in this very life.

When this Dhamma is investigated, understood, and realized, the delusion of *'I am'*, *'mine'* and *'my self'* that brought suffering throughout *samsāra*, is completely eradicated. Thus, one is liberated from the shackles of *samsāra*. This is the true deliverance.

Let us now analyze our lives. By not realizing the truth, we have travelled this long and sorrowful cycle of birth and death, with great suffering and pain. Due to ignorance and delusion we perceive *self* in what is not *self*. When we are caught up in this delusion, we view, perceive and think erroneously. These wrong views prevail in the world until the Supreme Enlightened One reveals the true nature. The Blessed One proclaimed how one can achieve deliverance from ignorance and delusion.

Don't Miss this Opportunity

After death of a human being, it is very rare that the subsequent rebirth is in a human plane. Similarly, it is very rare that a human being after death reappears as a deity in a good state of existence. The subsequent rebirths of many beings are in states that are non-human or in unfortunate states of existence. After death, most human beings reappear in a state of deprivation, in a bad destination, or in hell.

Supreme Buddha explained this with a simile. The Blessed One placed a little soil on the tip of a fingernail, and compared that to all the soil on this great Earth. The soil on the tip of the fingernail is insignificant in comparison to the soil on this great Earth. Even so insignificant, are the beings who reach perfect sanctity, the final liberation from suffering.

Therefore, it is clear that this is not something that can be accomplished effortlessly. Each individual has to put forth the necessary effort, and work out his own deliverance with mindfulness. A noble disciple, who possesses unflinching energy with firm determination to realize the Four Noble Truths, will be able to work out his deliverance.

Let's Live Close to the Perfect One, the Tathāgata

Suppose one leaves the household life and becomes a monk. He is wearing a robe just as the Tathāgata wore a robe, and walking just as the Tathāgata walked. Even if a monk should walk directly behind the Tathāgata, holding the robe of the Tathāgata, he will not progress along the path to enlightenment and final deliverance from the suffering of *samsāra*, if he is weak in determination and thought. He will not find the way to wisdom; the way to enlightenment. He would be considered to be living *very far* from the Tathāgata.

Yet, there may be a person who is physically very far away from the Tathāgata, but heedful, ardent and resolute, and therefore, he may find the way to wisdom; the way to enlightenment. He would be considered to be living *very close* to the Tathāgata.

The Doctrine is our Teacher

The Blessed One is not alive today. But, the Doctrine, which the Blessed One set forth, is alive. This Doctrine is our Teacher. Therefore, we must analyze the Dhamma with pleasant minds and with reverence as we worship the Tathāgata, the Perfect One.

If you would like assurance that this discourse that I explained to you today is conforming to the words of the Tathāgata, please refer to the *Ānāpānasati Samyutta* – Samyutta 54 in the Samyutta Nikāya. Personal views and ideas are neither interesting nor important to us. No one in the universe can be liberated from the fetters of *samsāra* without the Doctrine of the Blessed One. Therefore, the Dhamma is our refuge.

Breath Leads to Liberation from *Samsāra*

Now see, we have been breathing in and out right along as we discussed this discourse. Yet, we did not know that based on simple breathing, the mind could be developed to the final stage – the *Arahant* stage. The truth has been discovered and revealed by the Enlightened One.

Let all of us take up the supreme aspiration; the highest aspiration in the world that could be attained with a human mind. May all of us walk the path of virtue, concentration and wisdom, to shorten our sorrowful journey in *saṃsāra* and attain complete liberation – *the supreme bliss of Nibbāna!*

Sādhu! Sādhu! Sādhu!

May you have the opportunity to understand the Four Noble Truths in Gautama Sammā Sambuddha's Dispensation.

ᘓ *Ven. Kiribathgoda Gnanananda Thera, the Chief Monk's Journey Of Seeking the Noble Eightfold Path*

This time period is very fortunate for us. We are fortunate to have obtained a *rare* human life, during a very *rare* time in which Supreme Buddha's dispensation still exists in this world. If we don't realize how rare this opportunity is, we will continue to endlessly cycle through the rounds of birth and death in this *saṃsāra*. We will be re-born in hell, the animal world, the ghost world and in other unpleasant planes of existence. This danger has been explained very clearly by our great Teacher, to whom we have gone for refuge.

I'd like to share some facts about my life that are perhaps not commonly known. It is well known that I am not a Buddhist by birth. However, at the age of 6 months I took refuge in the Triple Gem and became a Buddhist. I'll describe how the incident took place.

My parents wanted to have a son, so they prayed incessantly, but a daughter was born instead. They continued praying for a son, and yet again a daughter was born. Again, for a third time, they prayed for a son, and once again a daughter was born. My parents were deeply saddened. One day, a Buddhist Upasika (lay devotee), Wimalawathie, came to meet my parents and told them to seek help from the Triple Gem. Accompanied by Uppasika Wimalawathie, my parents went to the Kiribathgoda Buddhist Temple and after paying homage to the Triple Gem they observed a vow to the deity Katharagama, asking for a son. Soon after, I was born. However, my parents did not follow the Dhamma properly. They continued to practise rites and rituals from their previous religion. Six months later, Upassika Wimalawathie advised my parents to discontinue their current practices as they were unbeneficial and to go to Katharagama Temple and fulfill the vow that they had made instead.

I can still remember the experience to this day. My father stood me up in Katharagama's Manik River at the age of six months. When we were near the Kiri Vihāra Dagaba, some kind of invisible power possessed my father and said, *"This son was born to your family in order to convert to Buddhism."* So that day, embracing me, my parents converted to Buddhism.

However, no one knew the purpose of taking refuge in the Triple Gem, and that the *real* purpose was to understand the Four Noble Truths. Since no one taught them these principles, they went to a mix of Catholic, Hindu and Buddhist temples, like many Buddhists in Sri Lanka at that time. Nevertheless, due to my good fortune, when I was sixteen years old, a thought occurred to me: *'This is not the correct way. Realising Nibbāna is the best way.'* I then received my parents' permission to be ordained as a monk.

Dikwelle Pannananda Lokuswaminwahanse and Seruwawila Sri Sumedankara Mahanayaka Swaminwahanse assisted me in training to become a monk. I was ordained at the age of seventeen, following these Bhantes' advice. First, I received traditional Buddhist academic education under the guidance of Seruwawila Saranakiththi Nayakaswaminwahanse, and then later enrolled in Jayawardhanapura University. However, I felt that my university studies were futile, and that *the truth* lay in attaining *Nibbāna* in this very life. There was a reason for this thought. When I was studying in university, I resided in a temple. There, I had the opportunity to read many discourses from the Sutta Pitaka. At the end of all these discourses, it was stated that many different kinds of disciples attained *Nibbāna*. Reading this brought tears to my eyes as I asked myself the question, *'Why can't we realise Nibbāna?'*

As the thought sunk deep within my heart, I began to find the Dhamma. Before completing the degree, I left university and became a recluse. Then I decided that I would go the Himalayas to seek the assistance of invisible powers.

I had traveled to India previously to learn Hindi, at which time I participated in a Buddhist pilgrimage. I worshipped at Varanasi and Buddhagaya, and then we started the journey to Rajagaha. However, while stepping on the stairs to Gidjakuta rock-mountain, a wonderful thing happened. A memory of a previous birth started flooding my mind. When I arrived at the peak of the mountain, I remembered that in a previous birth I had been practising the Dhamma as a monk with the Venerable Ananda, the Chief Attendant of Gautama Supreme Buddha. I was overcome with tremendous sadness in learning that I had lived such a life and associated with such Arahants, and yet in spite of that fortune, I was still unable to escape from the grips of *samsāra*. Having gone to the middle of the forest, I wept until the sadness left my mind.

I returned to Sri Lanka and dedicated my life to finding the *true* Dhamma. I would either go to the Himalayas and find the Noble Dhamma, or die on behalf of my attempt. I started to read discourses (*suttas*) with the pure intention of understanding this Dhamma for myself. While I was reading, I found wonderful and marvelous discourses. However, lay people did not have this opportunity to know about the Supreme Buddha's discourses, as people in Sri Lanka had lost confidence in these great Teachings. They had given up the Dhamma saying that it was a useless effort nowadays, and cannot be understood. Attaining the fruits of the Path (*maggaphala*) was a joke to many. They were under the misconception that one needs to achieve the perfections (*pāramitās*) in order to have any significant gain. Others alleged that before attaining the fruits of the Path, we must deal with more important worldly life issues, like earning money or raising children.

In this way, there was a wrong view among both lay people and monks that the Dhamma couldn't be realized in this life itself. It was very hard to find disciples in Sri Lanka with *saddhā* (unshakeable confidence in the Buddha, Dhamma, and Sangha). Instead of trying to understand the Supreme Buddha's Dhamma, they were more focused on large traditional ceremonies and celebrations.

I faced a lot of discouragement while trying to understand the Dhamma, but in fact the Dhamma has thousands of wonderful and marvelous discourses. In the *Acchariya-abbhuta Sutta (MN 123)*, the Supreme Buddha explains there are four wonderful and marvelous things in this world with the appearance of the Supreme Buddha and the Noble Dhamma. In this world, people find pleasure in attachment, take delight in attachment and enjoy attachment. But, when the Dhamma of *non-attachment* is taught by the *Tathāgatha,* people like to listen to it, give ear to it, and try to understand it. This is the first wonderful and marvelous thing that arises upon the appearance of a *Tathāgatha;* an *Arahant,* a fully Enlightened One. Generally people find pleasure in conceit (*māna),* take delight in conceit and enjoy conceit. However, when the Dhamma is taught by the *Tathāgatha* for the abolition of conceit, people wish to listen to it, they like to give ear to it, and try to understand it. This is the second wonderful and marvelous thing. People generally find pleasure with defilements, take delight in defilements and enjoy defilements. However, when the peaceful Dhamma is taught by the *Tathāgatha* for the eradication of defilements, people wish to listen to it, give ear to it, and try to understand it. This is the third wonderful and marvelous thing about this Dhamma. Lastly, people generally live in ignorance, are blinded by ignorance and fettered by ignorance. But when the Dhamma is taught by the *Tathāgatha* for the abolition of ignorance, people wish to listen to it, like to give ear to it, and try to understand it. This is the fourth wonderful and marvelous thing in this Dhamma.

If the Gautama Buddha's dispensation is to shine tomorrow, it's due to efforts to attain the fruits of the Path, namely, the fruits of: *Sotāpanna, Sakadāgāmi, Anāgāmi,* and *Arahant,* and not because of anything else. If we discuss and practise this Dhamma clearly, we will have noble disciples that attain fruits of the Path. Only then can the Buddha's Dispensation shine. The Supreme Buddha teaches us a *rare* path. It is the Noble Eightfold Path. If we could even just enter that Path, our problems and troubles would diminish significantly. Initially, there was a large debate about whether people could still realize the Dhamma in this Gautama Supreme Buddha's dispensation. Many thought that our one and only salvation was in the future Maitreya Buddha's dispensation. People had given up the Gautama Buddha's dispensation saying, *'this is unnecessary, as we will meet Maitreya Buddha in the future, listen to His Dhamma, and then we will realize Nibbāna and escape from samsāra in His dispensation.'* Some wish to become Buddhas themselves. I even wished this in the past, but the Supreme Buddha never advised us to wish to become a Buddha. He taught us to understand this Dhamma as *followers.* It was about twenty years ago that I began to have a strong belief that this Dhamma could be realized exactly the way Supreme Buddha had taught it. It was then that I decided to find the *true* Dhamma.

Though there were many places that taught meditation, I couldn't find even one place where they clearly explained the Teachings of the Supreme Buddha. In comparison, if asked today *'What did the Supreme Buddha teach?'*, many people will clearly answer by saying, *'the Four Noble Truths'*. But at that time, even I did not know this. We were learning *concepts*: concepts of Māra, concepts of *Nibbāna*, Buddha and nature, etc. If I was asked, *'What are basic teachings of the Buddha?'*, I would not have been able to answer this question.

I commited myself to reading the Supreme Buddha's original discourses, but I didn't have a clear understanding of where to begin to practise. Over and over, a thought occurred to me: *'Somehow, I must escape from samsāra.'* The prospect of being born again into this unwholesome existence worried me; it was not the fear of dying one day. If we are born, death is a guarantee – whether we like it or not. My problem was the uncertainty of my destination after death. This was the one major concern I had as a monk. In order to find the answer to this problem, I gave up my higher education, temples and friends. Then I studied the Dhamma through the association of various monasteries and institutions. But I still didn't have a clear understanding of what I should practise. So, I decided to go to India thinking that if I was in a forest, I would meet religious teachers (rishis) and they would advise me.

In 1994, I went to the Himalayas and thought, *'Let me offer my life in the name of the truth and seek my liberation. Perhaps, it will help me to realize the Dhamma in the next life.'* My only friend was a small Dhammapada book. For a few days in India, I associated with monks and rishis. Later I left them and stayed in a little hut, near the Ganges River. With the river floating down calmly, and the Himalayan Mountains in the distance, I started thinking as I sat on the bank of the river. I heard chantings of Bajan (ritualistic worship) for devas everywhere. Suddenly, I felt a deep loneliness. This thought occurred to me: *'I am a disciple of the Supreme Buddha; and I have gone for refuge to the Buddha by saying, 'Buddham saranam gacchāmi'. Oh, but I do not hear the sound of those sweet words here! And if I were to die in the Himalayas, is there the chance that I would be born in a place where the words 'Buddam saranam gacchāmi wouldn't be recited?'* But then again I thought, *'No, that won't happen. I am seeking liberation with an honest and sincere heart. I will not get lost.'*

I decided to go into the forest in the Himalayas. A friend, Rishi Rajakrishna, planned to accompany me to Chandabedi, a village one hundred miles from Rishikesh. From there, we would have to travel by bus, and a further ten kilometres by foot. There, lay a forest near the Ganges River that was known to have lions roaming within. So, I thought to myself, *'Let me go there and tear up my passport, and sit under a tree thinking about Supreme Buddha. Then a lion could attack me, so that in my next life I could realize the Dhamma more easily than I am today!'*

We needed to take the bus at 3:00 in the morning. The previous evening, I wrote a letter to our temple in Sri Lanka saying that I would never return to Sri Lanka. I prepared my robes, bowl and a few other things. At nightfall, a monk came to my hut and knocked on the door. When I asked for the reason, he replied, *"Our Guru has said that you should not go on this journey."* It occurred to me that the journey I had planned had been cancelled in order to save me, as no one there could have known about my plan to leave in the morning.

After a week or so, one early morning at 1:30am, while I was still half asleep in my hut, which was a 6x4 foot area, covered with plastic sheets and plastered with clay, I saw a person dressed in white entering the hut. He said, *"You're very sad, aren't you?"* I replied, *"Yes, I am very sad."* He then asked, *"Could you not fulfill the purpose of coming to the Himalayas?"* I replied, *"That's right, I could not fulfill the purpose of coming to the Himalayas."* He then asked, *"Do you believe that you will be able to find what you are looking for in the Himalayas?"* I replied, *"Yes, I think so."* However, he retorted, *"No, it is not here."* Thus, I immediately sought answers: *"Then where is it – that which I am seeking?"* He answered, *"It is in the Noble Eightfold Path!"* That was the very first time I had heard that phrase. I had never heard it from a human being. He said, *"Go and follow the Noble Eightfold Path. Don't stay here."* I quickly sat up on my bed, wondering and wondering: *'What's the meaning of this?'*

From that moment on, I abandoned the idea of seeking external help, from monks and rishis. I understood that I, myself, must find my own liberation and that no one could give it to me. I knew my refuge should be based on the Dhamma. I decided to leave the Himalayas. By that time, I had many friends there. I informed them and the monks that I was planning to leave. They asked why I was leaving and where I was going. I told them, *"I am going to Sāvathi."* They asked me what had happened, and what was the matter with me. I said, *"I have decided to abandon all of these things. Only I can find my own liberation."*

Having reached Sāvathi, I entered the *Ghanda Kutti*, the room where the Supreme Buddha preached the Dhamma. I felt a great sense of joy. Staying at Lankarama temple, I found many books of the Sutta Pitaka again, and began reading. However, now I was eager to attain *Nibbāna* quickly. I think this is the natural reaction of one who really sees the dangers of *samsāra*. I wanted to escape *samsāra* quickly.

I came back to Sri Lanka eventually and stayed at the Vipassana Meditation Center in Colombo. I used to read discourses alone so that I could try to comprehend them. However, I didn't have the intention to teach the Dhamma or to write books. My only goal was to escape from *samsāra* as soon as possible. In order to achieve this goal, I decided it would be more suitable if I went to the Siripada mountain-forest. However, there I wouldn't be able to find alms, so I would have to eat leaves from trees to survive. As I didn't know much about Siripada, I started seeking information. Then I got to know that there was a monk in Sripada forest named Badureliye Chandhima. The Bhante said, *"Yes, you can stay in the forest eating leaves."* The Bhante had lived in the forest for two years in a cave only eating leaves and never going into the village.

With the desire to lead a similar lifestyle, I went and resided there as well. One day, while going to the Erathna temple, I observed my precepts, and began to climb the mountain. There is a nice place called Varanagala on Kuruwita road. I stayed there approximately two weeks, and eventually left there with the intention of going into the forest. I used to travel during the off season and along the way I would chant *Pirith* (protective discourses). I saw footprints of a tiger and heard the sounds of elephants passing through the middle of the forest.

Finally, I arrived at the Holy Footprint of the Buddha on Siripada Mountain. There, we met a watcher who was very kind, had great *saddhā*, and treated us well. After spending two or three days there, when I was ready to go back down, I noticed that the road had been blocked. Some people had placed coconut branches across the road. I walked up close and wondered, *"What is this? I do not remember these coconut branches across the road when I was coming up. Perhaps this is a message warning me not to come to this forest.* So, I continued to descend the mountain.

I then got the opportunity to donate one of my kidneys. Following that time period, I decided that I must go back into the forest. So from the other side of the mountain, I went into the forest where other monks dwelt. While I was there, I realized that there are big barriers and obstacles, placed by *Māra* (the Evil One) to anyone who seeks liberation. I'm not going to go into detail about them, but while I was there, I understood them well. Later,

I became severely ill in the forest, and came down with high fever. Other monks advised against remaining in the forest as the conditions were too harsh. They accompanied me down to a cave where the climate was more suitable.

When I was in the cave, I received some Tripitaka books from Colombo through the help of a monk. While reading, a thought occurred to me: *'One day in the future, if I were to get the opportunity, I would like to translate the Tripitaka into simple Sinhala.'* Then I thought, *'I have faced so many obstacles on this path to discovery, perhaps I don't have enough good merit. How shall I collect merit to help me on this Path?'* I decided that propagating the Dhamma (offering *Dhamma dāna*) would be the best and most significant way that I could acquire merit. This is why I decided to teach the Dhamma.

There is no connection between seeking worldly gains, offerings, veneration or publicity, and my personal journey. I am not looking for those types of gains. My only goal is enlightenment. No one can satisfy me by giving money, land, dwellings and vehicles. I seek for my happiness not by *clinging*, but by *abandoning*. I returned to Colombo to teach the Supreme Buddha's discourses. Generally, people didn't have a great desire to learn, so I hung up a small sign saying, "Supreme Buddha's Discourses are being taught." My first program was on a Saturday afternoon at 3 pm. Only four people attended the first sermon and I started to teach the Dhamma to them. The same four people attended the following Saturday, and they continued to come for a month. Gradually, the news spread, and the number of disciples who came to listen increased. When the number increased to 200, the program was prohibited by the temple. So, the problem became finding a large enough space that was also calm and quiet. This would be the most suitable way to teach the Dhamma. I did not have any intention of building an institution of such, as this would defeat the purpose of my mission.

At the time I met Kotapala Amarakerthi Thera and he asked me to accompany him to Polgahawela. He took me to the present Mahamevnāwa site. At that time, it was an expanse of Eraminiya Strums. I did not know anybody in the village and there were no *dayakas* (lay devotees who would run and maintain a meditation centre). Amarakerthi Thera offered me support, and asked me to take charge of the place. It was a very quiet and calm place, so I thought that it would be ideal for meditation practice and to propagate the Dhamma.

In the beginning, I had to make a few sacrifices. I was able to build three huts with thatched roofs and walls of plastic sheets. In addition, there was a Dhamma hall (20 X 10 feet) with a thatched roof. And with those meager facilities, the Mahamevnāwa Meditation Monastery at Polgahawela was established. I organized a meditation program, and 25 people attended. Eventually, the number of people increased, and little by little, the Supreme Buddha's *true* Dhamma spread thoughout society.

Soon, the Dhamma started spreading beyond belief. My honest and sincere wish to spread the Dhamma was the enabler of this success. I understood the real Dhamma, as taught by the Buddha, and used a little creativity to propagate it. I preached to the Dhamma-seekers with sympathy, and convinced them of their wrongful attachments (devotion to astrology and auspicious times), which wasted their energy.

I used simple Sinhala to explain the Dhamma. I clearly explained the Four Noble Truths, which is essential to realizing the Supreme Buddha's Dhamma. Wise people gathered around and hundreds of young men came to me and asked to be ordained as monks. They took a profound interest in the Dhamma and earnestly learned the Buddha-Dhamma. This allowed for the renewal of the *true* Noble Dhamma, as there were now monks to sincerely teach the Dhamma to others.

Now we have about 54 branches of Mahamevnāwa in Sri Lanka and branches in foreign countries such as India, Canada, America, Australia, Germany, Dubai and England. There are about 600 trained Monks in these monasteries. The Mahamevnāwa started on August 14, 1999, and blossomed into a huge tree with strong branches, for thirteen-years. There was a big difference in how people understood the Dhamma, which was demonstrated in the questions that they asked. Now people ask about the Five Aggregates of Clinging, the Six Faculties, Dependent Arising, the Noble Eightfold Path, and the Four Noble Truths. Therefore, they have been able to accumulate a vast knowledge of the Dhamma.

So in this way, I wrote my first book, "Ae Ama Niwan Suwa Boho Dura Nowey?" This book spoke of the supreme bliss *of Nibbāna*, and about the four foundations of mindfulness – the *Satipatthāna Sutta (MN 10)*. The second book was "Ape Budhu Samidhu Thawama Wada Wesethi". It is the Sinhala translation of *Sutta Nipāta*, a very old book. I hadn't even heard of this book in my fifteen years of monkhood, so I doubted that any lay people had heard of it, eventhough it was chanted by lay people during the Supreme Buddha's life. My next book was about Dependent Arising which was named as "Wismitha Avabodhaya". Another book was printed named "Budhu Samidhu Daka Ganimu," which consists of some of my Dhamma sermons that were held in Colombo and recorded by a lay devotee. The next translation was the Dhammapada, translated into simple Sinhala, and a book for children called "Sigithi Lowata Budhu Samidhu Wadinawa".

Then I decided to translate the original discourses into simple Sinhala, beginning with *Majjhima Nikāya*-Part 1. While I was translating, I remembered it was the first book which I had read many years ago. Once when I was staying in a temple, there were big books of suttas, but I didn't have a proper understanding of what these books really were at that time. However, when I started to read these books, my life changed completely – in a wonderful way. I realized that *these* are the *real* discourses of the Supreme Buddha, and this is the Dhamma which should be realized; this is the Dhamma which is essential for life.

After that, I translated the *Majjhima Nikāya* - Parts 2 and 3, *Samyutta Nikāya* - Parts 1, 2, 3, and 4, *Khuddaka Nikāya* - Part 1, *Petavatthu and Vimāna Vatthu* (the stories of the ghost world and heavenly worlds), *Thera and Therī Gāthās* (the poems of Arahant bhikkus and bhikkunis), *Anguttara Nikāya - Part 1, Deegha Nikāya - Part 1*, and many more books.

As time passes, everything passes; everything becomes impermanent." I too have faced the world which is eventually subject to aging. By reading this autobiography, if you can identify me as an honest and sincere disciple, who seeks the ultimate liberation in this Gautama Sammā Sambuddha's Dispensation, that would be enough for me. "

Sādhu! Sādhu! Sādhu!

May you have the opportunity to understand the Four Noble Truths in Gautama Sammā Sambuddha's Dispensation.

Tanhā Janeti Imam Geham
Craving is the Builder

Anekajātisamsāram
Sandhāvissam anibbisam
Gahakārakam gavesanto,
Dukkhā jāti punappunam.

Gahakāraka ditthosi
Puna geham na kāhasi
Sabbā te phāsukā bhaggā
Gahakūtam visamkhitam
Visamkhāragatam cittam
Tanhānam khayam ajjhagā.

Through many a birth
I wandered in samsāra
seeking, but not finding
the builder of this house.
Sorrowful is it to be born again and again.

O house-builder! Thou art seen.
Thou shalt build no house again.
All thy rafters are broken.
Thy ridge-pole is shattered.
My mind has attained the unconditioned.
Achieved is the end of craving.

Gautama Supreme Buddha
Dhp 153-154

129

Abbreviations

Buddhist text references have been abbreviated as follows:

MN	Majjhima Nikāya
SN	Samyutta Nikāya
AN	Anguttara Nikāya
Kh	Khuddaka Nikāya
Dhp	Dhammapada
Ud	Udāna
Thi	Therīgāthā